AMONG
FRIENDS

AMONG
FRIENDS

A memoir of one woman's expectations,
disappointments, regrets & discoveries
while searching for friends-for-life.

MARY LOU SANELLI

An Aequitas Book
Pleasure Boat Studio: A Literary Press
New York

Sanelli, Mary Lou
Among Friends: A memoir of one woman's expectations, disappointments, regrets & discoveries while searching for friends-for-life.

ISBN: 978-1-929355-52-5
SECOND PRINTING
Library of Congress Control Number: 2008941466

Book Designed by Diane Rigoli,
Rigoli Creative, San Francisco, www.rigolicreative.com.
Cover Photo: Erik Reis

Aequitas Books
About the Press: Aequitas Books is an imprint of Pleasure Boat Studio: A Literary Press. We are located in New York City. The imprint focuses on sociological and philosophical themes in non-fiction. Pleasure Boat Studio books are carried by Baker & Taylor, Ingram, Partners/West, Brodart, and Small Press Distribution (SPD).

For more information,

Pleasure Boat Studio: A Literary Press
201 West 89 Street, New York, NY 10024
Email: pleasboat@nyc.rr.com
URL: www.pleasureboatstudio.com

PRINTED IN THE UNITED STATES

by Thomson-Shore, Inc.

Aequitas Books is a proud subscriber to the Green Press Initiative. This program encourages the use of post-consumer recycled content paper with environmentally friendly inks for all printing projects in an effort to reduce the book industry's economic and social impact. We are pleased to offer this book as a Green Press book.

Acknowledgments

For his continued support and good editing I wish to thank my publisher, Jack Estes. By now, Jack is more than my publisher. He is my friend. Thanks, too, to my book designer, Diane Rigoli of Rigoli Creative in San Francisco, who knows which fonts to use, and in what tone to offer advice. I am indebted to her for taking the time to imagine my books with me.

I would also like to thank my team of first readers: Jeane & Jackie & Sheila. I owe you three an enormous amount of gratitude for your time, help, and honesty. You nudged me forward. Again.

I couldn't have written this without all my friends (and ex-friends) who forgave me my flaws (or didn't) as I fumbled my way into maturity.

Among the best of my godsends is the generosity of the women who shared with me the fruits of their own friendship flubs, joys, and disappointments. I can still hear us talking together, reacting to each other, and the quiet after. And, see, I did not print your names if you asked me not to. Just like I promised.

I also wish to thank the David & Julia White Artist Colony in Costa Rica for allowing me to come and expand my thoughts for awhile. (Also, for removing the abandoned car from the field in front of my window so I, the fussy American writer, could see only the earth.)

And then there is Larry. Thank you. You define the word *friendship* for me. And: *love.*

Excerpts from this book have appeared in *The Seattle Times; The Seattle Post Intelligencer; Crosscut; The Peninsula Daily News; Art Access Magazine; The Queen Anne News; The Belltown News; City Living Magazine* (Pacific Publishing, Seattle); as well as aired on KSER FM; KONP AM; *Ladybug Live Radio,* and on *Weekend Edition,* National Public Radio.

CONTENTS

The straight path follows an endless curve.

— ALICE WALKER

Among Friends:
An Introduction

"Friendship is noble, 'tis love refined."

—SUSANNAH CENTLIVRE (C.1667-1723)

S itting here, fingertips linked to the keyboard, I wonder how I will put into words what it means to be a good friend, both in everyday ways and in ways vital to a woman's well-being. Ways that demonstrate that I at least have some understanding of what it takes to befriend someone well. I'm also wondering how I will make sense out of the hodgepodge of emotions common to anyone who decides to befriend another?

The answer is: I can't. But I *can* write about what has worked and, perhaps more importantly, what has not panned out for me in this realm of intimacy. And I can offer the stories of other women I talked to or exchanged emails with. I think experience is the most clarifying tool there is.

And though I don't believe the subject of friendship is of less importance to men, I want to speak directly to (and about) women because I can't begin to claim that I have the same level of entree into the minds of men.

1

But I'm no expert. I'm not a psychologist, psychiatrist, or psych-*anything*. I never added a doctorate or a master's degree to the fact of me. I work as a writer/speaker with the ordinary experience of workaday life at the heart of my subject matter.

And, unlike a scholar, I didn't consciously set out to make a study of friendship or to uncover what friendship may have to teach. More like, over the long haul between grade school and middle age, friendship, unknowingly, made a study out of me. In that sense, whenever I replay my life, I can hardly believe how idealistic I once was about my friendships. It's taken me years to slowly absorb and digest how ambiguous they can be.

For instance, each friend I make gives rise to a different part of me that needs to flourish. Yet if this newer bond causes a less satisfying friendship to fall away, a friendship that, at some point, forced me to accept the fact that *it just isn't working*, I'm demoralized even though relief is what I feel on another level.

I guess I still have a long way to go before I'm not overly tolerant of some of these friendships that, if I'm honest with myself, add nothing to my current life. I question myself instead of trusting the voice inside me yelling, "Oh dear God, please no!" when I hear her voice on my answering machine.

But why?

First off, it's not easy to move on. Ugh. I can find the whole process of letting go excruciating. Even though some friends I made as a younger woman no longer fit, I find the work of making new ones at this stage of life — when aging is sneaking up from all sides — no longer fully suits me either. When I meet someone I'd like to get to know better, I can have these big, awkward, unnerving moments of melancholy that are mixed with my hope for a new friendship. If I compare an emotional parting to pruning, I handle it better. I tell myself that a part of me needs to shed a branch now and again in order to thrive.

Secondly, I want to address the fact that sometimes the very mention of friendship can make my insides tighten and sink. This is when I really need to pay attention. Not because I particularly love the process — digging into ourselves can be exhausting—but because I find the whole topic necessary. And exciting. And terrifying. It's like that first roller coaster ride when you're a kid. You stare at it, scared silly. But you take the ride.

And I have no desire to instruct. Zilch. Or to write a "how-to." Good God, no. I'm just going to let my thoughts catch up to me, one-by-one. I want to take a hard look at the myths that surround friendship, is all, and try to take each out of the sentimental box they are usually wrapped in. You know, like when someone labels friendship between women *heartfelt.,* a word so banal it makes me shutter.

Not too long ago, a dear friend, a visual artist, asked me a question that caused me to take a deep breath and pause: "What does friendship look like to you?" I remember trying to stumble through an answer and not being able to formulate my thoughts. In a way, this entire book is an effort to answer that question more clearly.

Today, my answer comes easily: *I see laughter. Lots of it. And acceptance, of my friend and of myself, and a desire to learn from each other.*

Her next question was one more easy for a writer to work her way through: "What does it feel like if a friendship is working?"

Here is my answer, written in a style workshops call a "free-write" because you let the words fall without lifting your pen from the page: *We are ourselves and there is nothing to prove.*

And then I wrote: *Friendship is the opposite of loneliness, not aloneness, which I think women need more of, but loneliness. My marriage can't fill the void I feel when I'm at a loss for a girlfriend to laugh with. Some of my friends have been supportive. And not-so supportive. If I compared friendship to music I'd say it's a smooth groove mixed with a rap gritty as sand. And the sand is wet. So it slows us down. Good. Maybe then we'll be able to figure out how to move in sync without one or both of us falling on our ass.*

When I look up, I realize I didn't take a breath while writing those words. I laugh when I re-read them. I think they will always ease the tension I feel when, say, a friend says something that hurts and a part of me wants to distance from the bond for good. I'll remind myself that a time out from our waltz is okay.

So here I go. I'm going to plunge into this book about friendship.

Then I'm going to swim into it, way out over my head.

And laugh. Especially that. And especially at myself.

And I'll write about all of it.

JAR OF CARROTS — *for Meg*

When we were young, say, college age,
we swam together further and further
out into life, toward any rock
large enough to stand on.

Measuring my clumsy strokes against your grace
I came up short and envied you
that spring morning when it rained
until a sepia wash of earth slid right up to our door
of the dilapidated farmhouse we rented. Envied you
because you had the guts to skip class,
preferring to surface quietly
with a mug of tea and a book.

Years later, in my well-ordered kitchen,
there is this shelved jar of carrots, a refusal of sorts
to give up on us. Carrots you cut up
during our last visit that went so wrong:
Awkwardness undermined our reacquainting
until, though we stayed together, each of us left
for some other place.

I won't eat the fruit
that floats and bobs and pickles.

How long has it been? *I love you.*
Never said as much
but I've dropped my tough act
and say those words when I should.

Odd, don't you think, how much we used to talk
way into the night. Nowadays …

so much goes unspoken. Each rise of pleasure
we feel in our lives has nothing to do with each other.

We've stored our closeness away
like a tin of ornaments
to bring out later in life (I hope)
when we aren't so consumed
by motherhood, marriage, aging parents,
security, financial or otherwise,
or when we just want to
remember. *I think about you,*
I say to myself.

I think about you, too.

ONE

New Friends

*"All friendship between women has a uterine air about it,
the air of a slow exchange, of an original situation
being repeated all over again."*

—MARIA ISABEL BARRENO (1939-)

It occurs to me that when I'm bored or dissatisfied with certain aspects of my life, say when my work is going badly or the only living creature I can relate to is my cat ... the list reads on: When I feel stuck, unable to focus on what I *have* instead of what it is I think I want. When I'm overly compelled to do more and *be* more. When I can't seem to practice or even remember my rescue catchphrases: Failure vs. success is a moment-to-moment thing. Or: In the course of becoming there is no arriving (my personal favorite). Anyway, when I'm in this rubble of a mood, I sort of retreat from the world because I lose a sense of my 5-foot-2-inch self.

When I go limp in this way and don't take responsibility for what it is I need to change, self-doubt sits itself plunk down and I begin to see myself as a victim of my life rather than in control of it. The unfortunate outcome is that, now, I'm not only bored, I'm *boring*. I don't think of myself as a boring person, or I don't want to think of myself as a boring person, but as I fall into the grips of what I know darn well is boring*ness*, I start to criticize the very things about myself (oh ... and about my husband) that I normally love. And I know I'm at my lowest when I begin to attribute others, even my friends, with some of the dissatisfaction I feel, which is something I thought I might never be able to admit, but there it is. Whether this dip in mood is psychological or physiological, I haven't a clue, but, on the other hand, it doesn't really matter, does it? Because either way it feels awful.

Finally, one day something changed: I woke up, and for whatever reason, I could see how a large part of my ennui was fear. Plain old fear of nothing specific. Just of *every*thing. When it was happening, I just kind of froze. But I made myself listen. The day went on from there, a day that had a lot to teach me about how fear can make me spineless and resistant to the changes I know I need to make. And to the best advice I receive from friends, books, even my conscience.

That day was a signal that I needed to get back out in the mix, that a part of me had become too isolated as a writer and that I needed to shake things up, try something new, some*one* new. No, I'm not talking romance.

When we're younger, dating, of course, is directed towards finding a mate. We read magazines full of silly ideas that steer us toward snagging a date. But as we move on in life and become more confident in our sexual fulfillment (and even if we don't), I think a lot of us need to apply a few "dating" techniques toward the pursuit of friendship. And, as in dating, with all its uncertainty and embarrassing what-was-I-thinking-this-man-is-a-moron situations, we may also need to follow through with a *if at first you don't succeed* mind set in order to weed out the bad dates from ones good enough to pursue.

And, for the record, I have endured a few really bad dates.

No, truly, they were really bad. But that's the point. They were exactly what I needed.

Such as: A few years back, while visiting Manhattan, I looked up an acquaintance who lives in the city. We'd met months before at a writers conference in Seattle where we were both hired as consultants. Our meeting in New York was to be our official second "date." A friendship-spark had clearly passed between us at the conference, so, I thought, here's where my new mix begins! Ready. Set. Off I go.

I bought tickets to a production of a play entitled (and this is such a weird and funny coincidence) "Bad Dates," starring Julie White. It was the story of a divorced, middle-aged, shoe-obsessed, ebullient New Yorker who resolves to re-enter the world of dating. Staged at the Playwrights Horizons Theater, it was a cozy theater in keeping with most off-Broadway venues, seating about a hundred people.

Our seats were front row center. No more than ten feet from the actress at all times. Now, I agree the "lonely-heart in love with her shoes" theme of the play isn't the most original plot, but I thought the monologue was well-written and captivating. Because, passe or no, I, too, have a shoe addiction I have to keep under wraps if I don't want to be a high-heeled bag lady some day, so when the actress looked longingly at her favorite pair of Chanel pumps before propping them on her dressing table under a tiny spotlight, it tossed my sense of humor into the air. Only minutes into the play the purest appreciation swept over me. I was fully absorbed and it felt wonderful to laugh out loud.

Now, to all around us, *forget* the play. My embarrassing theater date was the real show. Appalled by the character, she made audible sounds of disapproval during the entire first act. Then, as soon as the lights went out for a scene change, she exclaimed, "This is not fresh! This is not funny! This is the worst play I have ever seen!"

I was horrified. My ears were on fire as I slid down in my seat. I wanted to pinch her and not let go, or shout, "Shut up and act like a normal person!" I sat there wishing I could click my heels together and make the whole evening go away.

Julie White kept her composure and never missed a beat. I have never admired a performer more. Still, what I found even more amazing was how my friend was tone-deaf to the disruption she was causing. I, on the other hand, felt like a ticking Geiger counter, so far on the other side of embarrassed that I came fully around to feeling calm. I had to. My only other choice was to rise from my seat and run.

That, I decided, was not an option.

Not only was I enjoying the play and paid a small fortune to be there, I was determined to ride the date out for my *research*, I told myself (at least a hundred times). Add that to the second reminder nagging me: Anyone who thinks they have the tenacity to write a book, better have the strength to ride out an uncomfortable evening.

As the lights came up for intermission, I could think of no snappy comeback to my friend's too-loud comment that the play was *"sooo* shallow" other than ... *for Christ's sakes, if you want deep jump down a fucking well!* Instead, I let her words sit without comment between us like the last wedge of Brie on a party tray.

But later, over dinner, we shared a good laugh about our polarized reactions to the play. And I was reminded that people are seldom, maybe never, just who we want them to be. I know some actions are unacceptable, but I could easily forgive her outbursts simply because she was willing to laugh at herself. I figured if she didn't care if the entire theater thought she was a nutcase, why should I?

Where we settle tells a lot about us. New York is full of colorful, opinionated characters. I looked over at my new acquaintance and thought *she is just one of them.* And later, when

I thought more about her high-stress career as an editor in a major publishing house, all at once it dawned on me that, in her mind, she was simply editing the play from the office of her seat. She was not, in the least, ashamed of her behavior. I'd done nothing wrong, so I decided to give myself a break and not feel embarrassed *for* her. Because I can do this sometimes: be a little too willing to take another's behavior to heart.

That evening showed me all over again that in order to make friends, keep friends, and *be* a friend I have to step back and view someone from more of a distance. *In order to see, you need perspective.* Who was it that said that? I don't want to peer in so closely, study it, so that I get lost in one bad behavior and become blind to the entire person. Because if we can't see beyond a few shortcomings, who will that leave us? Exactly no one.

I was relieved when, after the play and sitting in a sidewalk café on 46th Street, there was so much else about my friend's intellect and wit I enjoyed. I was satisfied with my first "date." I gained something positive from the evening. Good. Because the real me hates when her efforts turn into a total wash.

You don't have to read too carefully between the lines of this story to see how hopeful I was that evening. All of my desire was there: an attempt to get to know someone new, the first setback of the evening and then of my confidence, the turn-around of events so that a connection was finally made. As I left her to jump into my cab, my first thought was how much work it is to make a new friend. More important, I *liked* the work.

The dates rolled into one. For every one in a string of them that went awry, there was the one that flicked me into the good stuff. Here is where I like to remember what the visionary Doug Engelbart wrote, advice that sounds terrifying (because it is), but is also the kind of guidance I look for (I like my guidance to be like my body — short and to the point): "Your ability to grow in life is directly related to your ability to suffer embarrassment."

And the next time a woman triggers my interest, I'm going to step up to the plate again and ask her out for a walk, a drink, dinner. And not just for the sake of this book. I can't sit back and wait to be found. I'd never approach my work like this, so why should I my personal life? My motto is not original, but it *is* essential to the way I live: If I want something to happen, I have to *make* it happen. And prepare for it by working hard, damn hard, so that if and when it does come about I'm ready.

All this talk about friendship. It makes me question my choosing to be a writer, which means, ultimately, that I spend most hours of each day alone. Still, the voice inside me says, solitude is what, at the end of my workday, compels me to meet up with my friends. Sure, I like a lot of privacy, but I don't always bask in it.

But for women who experience a social swirl on a daily basis (office work, family), the subject of loneliness can be even more confusing. I talked to many bright, well-accomplished women of various ages who appear, from the outside looking in, to "have it all." Yet, underneath, most admitted that they are experiencing loneliness to some degree, or a lack of real friendship in their lives. I didn't want to turn our conversations into a political commentary on our culture, but still, we all seem to agree that something is wrong with our way of life. It's less complicated to understand why the elderly experience loneliness, but why at these earlier stages of fully-engaged life?

It's a tough question. Is it because we hold independence in the highest esteem? Which can make, either consciously or unconsciously, us view our most basic human quality — needing each other — as a weakness. Even if we pretend all is fine all of the time, each of us experiences similar emotions and needs. Whether it be jealousy, affection, fear, betrayal, doubt, or the alpha emotion: anger.

And, weird as this may sound, I believe in anger. Or, at least, recognizing it as true and finding a way to express it. I think channeling anger in the right direction makes for more satisfying relationships in the long run. Denying it, well, that just doesn't fly in my book, even if, while writing this, I'm a little concerned with setting an uneasy precedent. I know how far removed anger is from the near-desensitizing sensitivity that seems to be everywhere lately, making it difficult to speak out honestly. But I think in some circumstances (I'm thinking mother-big here: as in the complexities of family dynamics or love relationships) in order to initiate change, anger has to be met at the door and escorted in, not downplayed.

Now wait, *nothing* is acceptable about verbal or physical abuse; that's not what I'm saying. But anger as honesty, anger that stays focused on your own set of feelings, anger as a tension breaker, a release valve for the pressure cooker life can be. Why, I wonder, are we so afraid of it? Is it because we've had to bury it for so long so that we don't really know how to feel it? And why do we so often try to call it something else, as if getting angry implies something offensive instead of the strength it can be. Holding it back is unlike us. It runs contrary to who we really are. Certainly to what we feel.

I know we both get how things are: We get the message early on that if we express anger, people won't love us. It's such an affliction, all this self-censoring. I think it invites loneliness because we are not being ourselves. Sometimes it seems we're all just bluffing our way through.

In so many ways, men are allowed to get angry and still receive admiration and respect. He gets to be strong-minded while we are labeled *emotional*. His anger viewed as compelling while ours is interpreted as desperate. Part of me, the part that wants to give myself a break from trying to see life as fair, is willing to accept this as the way it is. But the other part, the larger part, still seethes ....

Sure, the women I spend time with express their anger. But most of us aren't all that comfortable with it. Not really. There is still so much guilt tacked on, and that's the part we go over and over in our conversations. I listen to my friends apologize for getting angry at their husbands, their friends, co-workers, or kids, even when the situation calls for it. As if anger is something to keep under wraps at all times. Even though we can see it right in front of us, like our own hand waving. If we don't allow it to surface, we have to repress it, right? And repression, as my massage-therapist says, "builds in us like dynamite. It's set to go off."

Just the other day I listened to my friend, a 37-year-old mother of a young son and a business owner, chastise herself for getting mad at her husband. When I asked what happened, I thought *thirty lashes to his backside would have worked for me, too.*

For months she'd been asking him to clean out his truck, their only transportation at the time. Whenever she tried to climb in, things would tumble out the door. And things went missing. Important things like his wallet, check receipts, keys. She was sure these items were in the mess that was the front and back seat of the truck.

Yet, to him the issue had become, "if the mess bothers you so much, then clean it up." But the reality of her life is that she is mother to a toddler, in the throes of opening her own clothing boutique and caring for her aging parents. Come on.

By now the missing checkbook was affecting their mutual life. But still her husband made no time to clean out the truck. He played golf, he played poker, but no clean-up.

She was forced to cancel their checking account and open a new one. Days later, while searching in the truck for a lost toy, she came across the check book she had pressed him to look for. That was, as the saying goes, her last straw. Her anger, she said, "had body weight." And why, I reminded her, would it not?

Later, as if on cue, she felt guilty. When she called, I didn't know what I would say that we hadn't gone over a hundred times before. Things like: Why do we find it so hard to let go of our real emotions? Aren't they our biggest strengths? But when someone is feeling really guilty, you can't go back and underline the important parts of past conversations. There is really little you can do to help. So I said to my younger friend, "I was thirty-five before I could express anger without crying, forty before I stopped apologizing for it. Especially to my husband." We laughed.

But, you know what, I'm not above this fall back. Not even close. I can easily retreat into the "good girl" dialogue of repentance (once a Catholic, always a Catholic) before I stop to consider what I'm doing. I can't seem to shake it entirely. I guess I'm still afraid of being labeled feisty, bossy, or bitchy if, in certain company, I don't cushion my anger with "nice." I fear I'll be judged harshly for giving voice to this emotion (I will be) which can end up taking a huge bite out of my self-esteem. So I hold back, censor what I say. But I need something more honest to build my friendships on.

Here's where I admit I have less and less patience for those who bring this hesitancy out in me, people who downright *refuse!* to get angry no matter what. New-age (what does that mean, really?) devotees — often sort of cranky, have you noticed? — who make a practice out of containing their emotions flat-out bore me. I can't blame them. In certain circles, especially in Seattle, "nice" has become too ingrained as appropriate behavior. But to me, too much of it seems out of balance, as if pursuing goodness swings people too far one way as much as drinking too much careens others. How are we ever going to bear the world's woes if we can't, at least, share an inappropriate giggle now and again? What, I wonder, is so nice about denying what you really feel if what you really feel is not all that nice? I don't think it's all that balanced if you've lost your sense of humor; that's what I'd shout from the mountain top. As one friend put it, "Eventually, you gotta show your dark side or it's dull, dull, dull!" When I find myself in this kind of careful, I can feel my tolerance oozing over the sides of me like a fallen souffle. I have trouble keeping my irritation to myself.

But I'm not *completely* unsympathetic. I understand when it's a culturally born detachment — think Scotch-Irish (I am), or any background where the personal or *inappropriate* isn't readily discussed either within or outside the family — how difficult it must be to pass one's past on, its scars. But, as any Italian woman who has taken a WASP for a husband can tell you, understanding something intellectually doesn't mean you can easily (or always) apply it emotionally. Too long in the company of someone afraid to risk (in conversation or in life) and I'm secretly hoping for a pressurized emotion of some kind to rise up and burst them open like a blow hole. Sometimes, usually after my eyes have glazed over, I prod, which is one of my many character flaws, just to try and free their habit of holding back.

And once I went so far as to look directly into my own eyes in the mirror and make a vow that I would never ever befriend another ex-Midwesterner or Presbyterian. I get too distracted by what I sense lies underneath, pacing but not poking through, as if restraint rises like a blister before me. And though I tell myself *don't pick, don't pick,* I am pathetically unpitying. And ribbing. And blunt. God help me, I get out my needle, pass it through the flame, and move in for the stab.

Suffice it to say, there are many attributes to my character I am not especially proud of. Maybe by the time you read this, I will have learned to walk away with a nod rather than prod, like a full-fledged mature person.

At a woman's retreat a couple of years ago, I was asked to give a talk about "living one's passion." That was the theme of the entire retreat, and I thought that would be good. The kind of women who would attend, it seemed to me, would be those who don't feel that they are living their passion, who won't or can't give themselves permission to. Even under normal, non-workshop/retreat circumstances, unsatisfied people can be a particularly receptive audience. But, at the same time, authenticity-seekers can be tough nuts to crack open in conversation. They've spent so many years in a holding pattern, not making the genuine connections they now crave. Or they can blather on and on, a little too eager to hear themselves talk, which is not making a connection, either.

When I finished my talk, I sat next to a woman who had clapped for me with her arms way up over her head, so I thought she'd be easy to talk to. Or, at least, receptive. She also wore a pin that read, "Passion is as passion does," which made me stop and think *huh?* but I still thought *good for you, honey!* But then I couldn't get her to open up about one single thing all during lunch. *It's not like I'm asking for a play by play of your sex life,* I thought, *or how big your savings account is, but give me something other than a rundown of your kid's life.* I'm embarrassed to say exactly how fast I ate my lunch.

My point is that in order to flourish in the company of another, we have to be willing to share the truth of ourselves, to reveal doubts, insecurities, fears, what disappoints and angers us. We have to try — please try — to reach beyond a display of ourselves. It's not that I want to wallow in what disappoints (I don't) or let anger bury me (absolutely, I don't), but I do want to speak from a true place. And to get angry if I need to. To quote my friend Gale, "I need to be able to have a hissy-fit now and again. I need friends who let me do this without assuming I'm a negative, fed-up person. It's my way of exhaling."

I talked with a woman who works at the corporate level of the traditionally male-dominated bastion of journalism. At the time I was writing for *The Seattle Times*, for the Job Market section and, for the first time in my life, I came to understand how a writer could, in fact, come to hate writing, and detest her job. It was so consuming, so thankless, so frenzied and demoralizing. But it was my *choice*. I didn't need the work. I thought it was "prestigious." And in some circles it was. Oh, the lessons we learn.

Sorry, I didn't mean to take that turn.

Anyway, I sat with her in her cubicle as she waited for a fax to feed through her machine. She is forty-one, short-haired, and intense. We talked about the conflict she often experiences at work: a struggle between her intuitive way of relating to the world and the acceptable way she needs to express herself within the rather rigid workplace.

We know the work place is not the smartest place to confide in someone anyway, or where we should expect or hope for unqualified loyalty from our associates. (Some of us have learned this the hard way.) Yet, the very layout of the office space with its tiny cubicles tempts our basic human tendency to be intimate. Proximity invites confession. Confession is the quickest means to intimacy. What a gnarl of juxtaposition versus closeness to wade through on a daily basis. It's hard, really hard, to unravel this tightly held knot when you leave the office and want to connect to the world on a personal level.

It's all so nuts these days, isn't it?

I found another kind of loneliness true for a few women who live in suburban developments. Especially once their children are raised. What seems to be missing from their lives is a sense of community, often more obtainable in a smaller town or even in the hub of a larger established city with its tightly meshed, multi-generational neighborhoods. True, they have the luxury of a private home, but is the trade-off their feeling more confined than ever?

A few years back, my sister moved from Brooklyn to a suburb on Long Island. She admitted to me that life is lonelier now that she bought her "dream" house. After several years in her new home, she has befriended only one neighbor. One. "And *that* acquaintance was forged," she said, "because our dogs found each other and wanted to play."

We laughed. I could do this, laugh everyday with my sister if only we made time for it. It is so comforting and familiar, the overlapping of us.

When she first told me she bought the house, I wanted to say what I'd recently learned, that dreams and dream-*houses* are polar-opposites; that dreams come from within *us*, not from our houses. I wanted to say that, but I didn't. I didn't want to spill on my sister's dream. Who wants to be afraid of what others will say about their dreams? Sooner or later, though, I think my sister will redefine her dream and move back to the city.

Leslie lives in a suburb of Seattle after fifteen years in an apartment in the colorful, inner-city neighborhood of Capital Hill. She said she always wanted a yard but now she feels isolated and soft.

"What do you mean by 'soft'?" I asked.

"I don't walk anymore. It's all about driving now. On my walks in the city I used to meet people, stand on the sidewalk and chat about the neighborhood, get the word about local politics. People aren't as open out here. There's no community. That's a suburban myth. Everyone pulls their car in the garage and goes inside. I don't care about lawn maintenance and school districts. And no one ever stops by. I miss that, my neighbors sticking their heads in my door. No one tells you about the loneliness. Look around when you drive out of here. You'll see pricey outdoor chairs everywhere but no one sits on them. After commuting, no one has time."

"Will you move back to the city?" I asked.

"Soon as the market comes around again."

"Will it?"

"Who knows?"

"Will you wait?"

"It would feel really good if I could say 'no.' Want to buy my house?"

There was a pause. And then this came to me: "A cul-de-sac is a dead end in more ways than one." I wrote that awhile back about my mother's move from her inner city neighborhood to a cul-de-sac in rural Connecticut.

Leslie looked at me and nodded. "Now, *there's* a description for the neighborhood newsletter," she said and we laughed. "Even though there's no neighborhood. Or newsletter. It's an email from some woman I've yet to meet."

I find these little moments, two of us poking fun, my favorite part about writing this book, about life.

After I left her I pulled my car over to the side of the road to write this: I remember growing up in a place like this. I feel the same impulse to run, to leave it behind. If I lived here I'd feel the peer pressure I felt in highschool. I see the weedless lawn, the acceptable color to paint the house, the nondescript clothes women wear to be seen in but not *noticed*, and I panic. Suburbs are such a strong equalizer. In my own life, I find a strong connection between aloneness and freedom. But aloneness is not ... *this*. This new development looks lonely to me. I feel more loneliness here than I ever thought possible.

I continued writing: If this is what is passing for community these days, it's only a matter of time before even our mortuaries are located in the nearest strip mall. (When I said this to my sister she said, "There *are* mortuaries located in the nearest strip mall. Where have *you* been?")

I'll say that every home standing alone may still be the American dream but it makes it hard to admit that you are in need of *any*thing. Whether it be a cup of sugar or a friend. To live where you need to drive miles and miles to any place that gives you a sense of community — well, just think of the time spent coming and going. Which leaves little time for much else. "I'm surprised how exhausted commuting leaves me sometimes, how vacant I feel when I get home," my sister said. Something has to give.

I think the first thing to give is the time we once had for friends. As the writer Judith Viorst put it: "The suburbs are good for children, but no place for grown-ups."

Or as my friend Jeane revealed: "I didn't have friends when I lived in suburbia, I raised my kids there. I took long baths and I cried a lot."

I know you realize I'm not proposing that everyone pack up their three-bedroom, two garage home and move to some small town in Idaho or a condo in the city. It's just that, no matter where we live, I think there is more we can do, more lines we can cross, to improve our emotional connections if we're just willing to reach past our four walls and get to know who lives around us, one-on-one (which is key for me; otherwise it's socializing, which is something entirely different). Because connection comes slowly, incrementally, no where near as fast as the construction that builds houses. It takes work, the emotional hard work of reaching out, to turn a development (or a city block, or a small town if people are new to it) into something that can hold people together.

Because I think ... I stop writing for a moment ... I *believe* that the kindest thing I can do for myself, no matter how busy I am, is to maintain my working friendships. And I want a new one now and again because I like how it feels to get another sense of myself, and enough old ones to keep me connected to my oh-so-old self.

One more thing: I just received an email from one of my dearest friends, Sheila. I sent her this opening chapter for a little feedback, you know, to quell the fears every writer has, fears that whine on about how, for God's sake, the world doesn't need another book. Certainly not mine.

Upon finishing the first chapter, the hardest one for me, instead of feeling relieved, I was bummed, wound up, and fidgety. Here's what she said: "As an artist I am accustomed to and need time alone. So it came as a surprise to me to realize that, recently, at the end of my day, because I've lost touch with several friends, one especially dear to me, there is *this* problem now. I'm lonely. And here you come with your book about friendship."

I write back that, yes, the thin line between aloneness and loneliness is exactly at the center of what I'm saying. (So maybe there is room in the world for just one more book after all.)

The poet in me would say it like this: Releasing myself in friendship is the silver dollar, the rare and worthy thing I want to hold onto. The realist? She's shown me, repeatedly, how a friendship that works is key to my sense of well-being, many times more than family ties. So, she's going to put it more like: *Listen, Miss I'm-So-Busy. You can pretend all you want, but no one wants to go it alone.*

Or something like that.

MEETING FOR LUNCH — *for Seth*

As the sun climbs to mid-day
we share food, a little gossip
harmless enough.
Nothing too trashy.

When young, you say, you looked to others
to measure your own merits by. To this day,
your self-esteem is temperamental
and I think how difficult it is to release the past,
that web of fear holding firm.

After you describe me to me:
a gust of getting things done, I say
its my father's fault. His work ethic
ironlike in me as the pile driver
hammering in the distance, a sound driving us
to drink up, bustle into farewell, and return
to various selves, concerns, the push
it takes to earn one's way.

Recently, I lost a friend.
She and I went searching for women
other than the ones we'd become.

I think of her, walking with you
on my arm, companion completely. My heart grows
no larger than this.

Once, you and I shopped together, hours
in artificial light. *Boys will be girls*, you said,
and we laughed from that safe place
two can share when they aren't afraid.

You needed shoes, suit, even a hat.

Surrounded by so much to buy,
we grew weary, bickered briefly,
until laughter leaned in, nudged our words,
and made ones not exactly kind ...
kind.

TWO

The Truth About Honesty

"What is more arrogant than honesty?"

—URSULA K. LEGUIN (1929 -)

"If you're going to be totally honest it's a hire-wire act. You better be ready to fall." Re-reading this quote, I vaguely remember jotting it down in my little notebook. But I do remember its message coming to pass in my life.

In the days after finishing the first chapter, I started to think a lot about the word *honesty*. Mind you, a periodic dose of checking in on the word is not a bad thing. For what use is a writer if she isn't honest? This is a question I struggle with a lot, though not as often as I did when I was younger and still grappling with the most powerful inner censor: the fear of not being liked. Once my teacher in college said that defeating this censor would be my greatest challenge in life. That pretty much sums it up for me.

By nature, I wrote once, *writers will cling to an individual honesty. Clearly why regimes kill us off first.* I was addressing (in one of my columns) how hard it was to publish my thoughts and fears about war in the aftermath of September Eleventh. I wrote the piece after I read that, throughout history, writers were thrown into prisons and condemned to death.

Now, this is even scarier: The Salem Witch Trials were, according to some, a cleansing of honest women, women who questioned whether the existing state of affairs should be *their* state of affairs. Apparently, all that domestic drudgery was supposed to keep us from thinking.

"If I lived back then, they would have burned me up," I said to my husband.

"Like a marshmallow, honey," he replied, a little too quickly. I have no idea why.

My friend Jeane came over the other day and brought the most amazing bottle of wine. It felt so good to stop writing and to pull up lawn chairs for a proper visit. I asked for her thoughts on honesty, and she said something so helpful it brought tears to my eyes, that, as we get older (she's ten years older than I am) there's no time for anything *but* honesty. "Honesty is all that matters," she said, "but maybe what I really mean is *trust*." She also said that, as far as she was concerned, I was one of the most honest people she knew. "Gee, if you weren't, I wouldn't waste my time sitting here. Now where's the damn corkscrew?" I breathed a sigh of relief. Sometimes I am absolutely blown away by *us*. And by how happy it makes me that we are past, way past, the kind of getting-to-know-you conversation we used to share.

Of *course* honesty matters. Even if most everything around us says otherwise: Think Hollywood, for starters. And politics, religion, Madison Avenue, and New Agers telling me that yoga and a colon cleanse will bring about a higher consciousness. Please.

We're raised with all these lies — all the things people say but don't mean — and told to tell the truth. I mean, it's all so crazy. I wonder sometimes what kids see when they look up to us. Do we seem truthful to them? Do they wonder, when they ask us a question about something serious — sex, say, or why people cheat — if we even know how to answer without telling some little lie to make the unexplainable easier on both of us? Do they see right through us? Our lies?

I've spent years going over the story I'm about to share. And whenever the guilt returns — the approach of that terrible feeling — I remind myself that I had the guts to be honest, sure, but it would have taken as much nerve to say nothing. But I had to learn that the hard way. And then I had to forgive myself for the blunder.

But it took me awhile. Forgiveness, especially *self*-forgiveness, never happens when I want it to. It makes its way in slowly. It takes its sweet time. All through my twenties and thirties I thought I could sweep it along quickly. But I don't feel that way anymore.

Looking back I think most of my misconceptions about honesty were (are) the result of my imagination. This isn't the worst thing, really, but it has gotten me into my share of trouble now and again. I watch too many movies. I used to watch too much TV. Way too much Oprah. It fact, once it seemed so believable to me that if Oprah saw Gayle's husband with his arm around another woman, a much *younger* woman — and much *prettier* woman — she would tell her pal what she wit-

27

nessed and their friendship would survive, intact as their hands and feet. *Vive la friendship!* Ditto for Carrie Bradshaw and her forgive-all four. (More on Carrie and friends later.)

Well, if wishes were fishes. Because real life has been a different story for me. I'm still cinematically misinformed, yes I am, but I'm working on it. Even so, I still *want* to believe in the movie version, the make-believe, the cubic-zirconia. But I can't. I've found out that it's not even remotely possible that cubic-zirconia is ever a diamond. No matter how lustrous it appears.

And yet, a part of me clings to the notion of life's happy endings, that if I do the steady work: tell the truth, play fair, extend generosity, I'll be graced with the very qualities that make life turn out beautifully. Like good muscle tone if I stick to my free-weight regimen. And isn't it great, wonderful, fantastic when things do work out and we are straight-away transported to the next best place in our life? Except, of course, when they don't and we aren't.

"I became a columnist because of questions like these," I once said in a radio interview.

"And have you answered many?" the host shot back.

I smiled, but of course my audience couldn't see that. "I'm not sure," I said without thinking. "I usually end up asking another."

"You answer life's biggest question then, it seems to me."

She was right. I do.

Unlike my Oprah/Gayle fantasy, when I told my friend about her husband's affair, I realized in an instant that people will, in fact, blame the messenger. I always thought that was the goofiest saying. I know better now. When no one is at fault but ourselves, we sure as hell want to blame *some*one. It's tremendously protective.

I stood there and watched my friend struggle with this worst-case-scenario (for wives) and for somewhere to put the anger surging through her nervous system like a double Scotch. When I reached out to hug her, she stepped back. She didn't say anything at first. But people don't have to speak to be heard. After the longest pause she finally said, "You *never* liked him." Then she shot me a look that burned through my eyes and pretty much cremated my self-confidence. Whenever I remember that look, which is often, I still feel something happening to me, like crashing waves breaking over my body.

This is what happened: While riding the ferry that whisks commuters from downtown Seattle to Bainbridge Island, I saw my friend's husband on the car deck with his arm around another woman (*not* a friendly hug). At that moment, it did occur to me to say nothing. To let it *go*. Be free of the responsibility. I know from experience it's possible to hold on to this kind of secret: Years back I'd stumbled on another friend's husband having an affair when she was out of town. Thinking she was to return a day earlier than was true, I went to her door, a bouquet in hand. What I found was her husband rolling on the living room floor with a hippie-girl in a tie-dyed T-shirt and no panties. I peered in, gasped, and ran away, pausing only long enough to throw my flowers back at the house as if *that* would show him. Silly, yes, but it's all the ammo I had in me at the time. (I promise to follow up with the outcome of this affair.)

But this time, for whatever reason, I didn't heed my own warning. God Almighty, who knows why. Instead, I trespassed, acted in spite of my fears (apparently *not* the definition of a hero) and told my friend what I saw. And with each word, I could feel our friendship grow more and more complicated. As if we were, suddenly, as stable as one of my father's humongous canning tomatoes hanging from a paper-thin vine, only a matter of moments before it gives. I waited for a signal (a nod, anything) that would have made me feel less like a tattletale and more like a concerned friend.

Overnight, literally, the present of our friendship became the past. We went silent, the worst kind of unraveling. We knew so many ways to chat about nothing, no topic too small or too serious, but silence we had never shared. I told my husband, "I wish I'd driven around Puget Sound that day and not taken the damn ferry."

"What's going on with the two of you?" he asked.

"What's going on with the two of us? Absolutely nothing." And how could I feel a little better? For starters, I could talk about wishing I'd kept my husband-cheating-sighting to myself, which, initiated by my better half, is what I did.

"I still think you did the right thing," he said after I was done (and done in) by going over the whole *should I have told her* scenario all over again.

"Would you have told her if you saw what I saw?" I asked. "No."

I knew it!

This is the stuff I rarely talk about: I felt the breakup in my shoulders. They became two rocks on either side of my neck. I sobbed. God, I felt tired. And lonely. I had no other choice but to move on. But it felt like I had shackles around my ankles. My steps were slow and heavy. *After all the years we've supported each other, don't I have a right to expect her to call me?*

Then again, I think, even if she had called me, or I had called her, our relationship would have inevitably shifted anyway. Relationships change during a crisis. They just do. Sometimes for the better. Sometimes not. I tried to be patient. I thought about how crappy things must be at home for her. *But, man, we really need to get to the conversation the two of us need to have.* Or *I* needed because guilt was getting the best of me. But why? (I still can't answer this question and it irks me.)

I also thought about something that had never occurred to me before, not really, or not in the serious sense (I'm not talking about whether you should answer honestly questions like "do I look fat in this?"), that, between friends, there can be too *much* honesty. And it can transform into too much awkwardness.

Which is exactly what happened between us.

Why don't I call? Weren't there things you just *did* when you're friends? I thought about this over and over and over. Then I'd swallow my pride, try calling, chicken out and hang up. *And say what?* I wondered aloud. *That I was sorry?*

Was I sorry? This kept digging at me. I was sorry she had an ass for a husband. But was I sorry I told her he was cheating? Yes. No. Yes. I don't know.

Ultimately, she forgave him. I learned this from a third party.

"Don't expect to be rewarded for telling the truth." This I read in an article geared toward writers. But the same is true in friendship, I think, unless the bond is out-and-out exemplary. (And I still believe there are out-and-out exemplary friendships out there, even if mine was not one of them.) Losing my friend became an opening I had to fill at a time in my life when I thought that kind of work was behind me.

How easy it is for me to admit how little faith I had in her decision to mend the marriage. I never got the opportunity to tell her that I, surely, could *not* forgive him. But I'm sure she knew. I'm also sure it's why I never heard from her.

Frankly, I don't know what kind of friend this makes me. One truth of me is that I don't get over things like betrayal very well. Even if it happens to someone else. The way my friend's husband flirted was an inside joke in our town. *If he betrayed you once, he's likely to do it again.*

Definitely what I'd be thinking. And definitely *not* good for our friendship. How could she hang in there with him without letting me fall away? Why would he want her to hold on to me if he thought I could see straight through him?

"It takes so little to come between people." A year before she died, I heard Eartha Kitt say this at a concert she gave at Jazz Alley in Seattle. And it's true. And it's almost too much to think about.

I was a younger woman then, and maybe that's the point; that's exactly why I couldn't see how fragile some ties are. I still thought friendship was a given simply because we had shared so much. I had to force my self to accept this fragility, the fine balance, so that I wouldn't resent the hell out of it.

To this day, I ask myself over and over the million-dollar question: Would I want, under the same circumstances, to know the truth? And each time I ask it, I think I finally understand what it is that comes between friends at a crucial time like this: Yes, I would want to know the truth. But only if my own instinct led me to it. I think maybe this is the real lesson I was supposed to come away with.

I called a local psychologist, Esther Conway, just to get a little professional savvy on all this. This is what she emailed back to me: "When one friend is forced to listen to the truth of her life relayed from another, even when that observer is a trusted friend, it can usurp the balance of the bond, which is supposed to be between equals, and leaves the unfortunate person feeling devoid of a good sense of judgment and, consequently, lessened. This level of honesty puts someone at a superior level. It tends to unbalance a relationship. It's not honesty shared two ways. Instead, it forces someone to see something they might be opting to ignore."

Oh.

Esther told me something else, too, a conclusion I'd already come to and was still trying to accept: that I would forever be the blatant reminder of the truth my friend and her husband needed to put behind them. That made sense to me. Eventually I pulled myself up, shook myself off, and walked on, emotionally speaking.

After this friendship, one I relied on for so many levels of satisfaction, broke apart, I felt disillusioned by the idea of friendship. I became friendship shy. And shyness is not something I do normally. It's way up there with saying no to a slice of cake.

About a year later, I heard through the grapevine that my friend's marriage broke up, that *she* finally left *him*. To this day, I wonder if she will appear on my doorstep or phone to say she regrets walking away from our friendship with the same stride she must have used to walk away from her marriage.

Nor have I reached out to her. I think the longer we let these things go, the harder they are to retrieve. Yet, if she were to appear, I wonder if we could reestablish our connection. Would we feel too forced? In the movie version, the scene would fade into slow motion and cut to hugs, tears, forgiveness. But, truthfully, I don't miss her in the old way that I did. I let go. I've forged new friendships that put the heart back into me.

Because when I finally stopped carrying the weight of letdown around so that I did, in fact, look like I just lost my best friend, I challenged myself to connect again.

Now, when I think of her, I don't get that squeezed feeling in my chest. I feel nothing but a little yearning for a part of my life that is no longer. Just like when I think about my once-taut tummy that's gone a little soft.

Sometimes you have to travel a long way to get back to the beginning. Now I keep my promise: Yes, I did hold onto the other infidelity-secret I revealed to you earlier. For fifteen years! And, yes, I finally told. But only after my friend had divorced her husband-the-cheater. Not because I wanted to rat on him (though it was a relief — admittedly a big relief). But because she was full of self-loathing after the divorce, thinking she was to blame for their failed marriage. It was then that I had to speak up. I'm right now trying to remember what her reaction was, though I'm not trying all that hard. Disbelief, I think. Mixed with relief.

But I never once thought about telling her back then, when we were younger friends together. I knew enough about the nature of our relationship to recognize that my telling would have been the straw on our backs. We were in our late twenties, still wrapped up in competing for who's-got-the-best-life; unable to face the truth of ourselves, our mistakes and faults, in the way we can now.

This is what I like to think anyway. My mother says I think too much. "Give yourself a break," she said to me yesterday. She's right. Sometimes my mind feels like a bulletin board poked with a pad full of yellow Post-its.

In a similar situation, I don't think I'd be honest again.

Those words belong to a ballet instructor. I met her at a café near the ferry landing on Whidbey Island. My notes say that sun was streaming through the glass above our table, filtering through the pattern of highlights in her hair, casting a reddish tint over our table, all of which have nothing to do with her story. But everything to do with why I love telling one.

She was happy to share her story. Women have a lot to say on the subject of friendship. More so when it goes awry. I hardly met anyone who didn't want to tell me exactly how she felt. Each woman became a support for me, a span connecting my story to theirs. And each time I left one of them I thought, hey, now I can look in the mirror and see both of us.

In one of her dance classes, a teenage girl, whom she sensed was headed for trouble, repeatedly came to class with reddened eyes. She would also cry uncontrollably after the slightest reprimand, or curl up in the fetal position in the back of the room and sleep. The problem was magnified, she said, by the fact that the student's mother was an old friend of hers, "ever since highschool."

I made an appointment to speak with both parents. Only my friend showed up. When I said I thought her daughter had a drug problem, she called me a meddler and pulled her daughter out of my class. The worst part was she said unkind things about me in the community. We live in a small town. People gossip. Things get around. Especially untrue things.

Weeks later, the young girl nearly died of an over-dose.

She still looks away when we run into each other.

I asked her if she was faced with this kind of situation again, would she handle it differently?

I don't know. Unfortunately, I have more empathy for teachers who don't want to get involved and just sort of turn a blind eye, figuring it's up to the parents to save their kids.

My thoughts when she was finished? How many ex-friends do we see and pretend *not* to? Each of them is our history, and we can't rewrite the past. And if you live and work in the same town you grew up in, none of it goes away.

For years, along with all the movies and TV, I was devoted to watching *Sex in the City.* Then I watched the re-runs. I've seen the movie twice. Next time I'm down with a cold, I'll likely rent it again.

Yes, I know the whole pretense of complete friendship, unshakable commitment, and dedicated loyalty is an illusion. Talk about cubic-zirconia. But maybe something else is at play, too, in all those episodes of super-supportive women not competing with each other. I know this "something else" is what I tune in for. To paraphrase a review I read about the series, a comment that's been circling in the back of my mind for years: Somewhere, lodged in our female cognitive memories, we must carry a recognition of a time when females relied on each other for their very survival.

Maybe this explains my addiction to the show, and why I am writing out my feelings about it. Because now, suddenly, I see it from the point of view of a woman looking back at her more cinematically-misinformed self.

Other than the fact that I'm New York-ish and a columnist, I watch because I adore how the four women support, care for, and talk honestly without hurt feelings. I want that kind of openness and verve, that New York City *hutzpa,* those conversations! I want to speak and live that story. Every time I watch, the unreal becomes my desire. And the unreal is an impossible standard.

The Portuguese have a word for it: *Saudades:* A sense of memory for something that might not even exist; still, you long for it all the same.

And I do. I long not only for the forthrightness and liveliness now that I live in Seattle, a city full of people who need their space — maybe because there's still plenty of it. I long for the kind of friendships that meet once a week, rain or shine, to synch up emotionally.

There's such an persistence behind my want of their closeness. I moved West without the comfort of family, so I carry around a fear of being without people to lean on through the rough patches. I'm always looking to find more of a family for myself, however family is defined circa 2009, who can offer the intimacy (especially around the holidays, no surprise there) I feel lacking in my life even though I'm blessed with a long-standing marriage and enough friendship to sustain me.

I might as well admit here that I don't think being as honest with my friends will ever be the reality. And this admission may be at the heart of Carrie and her quartet's success. But I'm pushing the envelope. And at this writing I have a few that come pretty close, graciously, which is deeply reassuring. And I'm finding others who are in need of surrogate family as much as I am, and a few who demand more honesty from me. (They are my favorites.) I'm so glad I kept looking. And that I no longer idealize what friendship should feel like. Or if I do, I'm able to stop myself before it festers. It feels as if my friends and I come pretty close to saying exactly how we feel and precisely what we need pretty much most of the time.

And, well, we are about as good together as real life gets, I think. We make life so much more satisfying. I suppose it's what people mean when they talk about well-being. This is what it's like to be content.

I was going to end here, had taken the first step to ending here, only to find I *couldn't* end here. All of a sudden this next story, a story I knew from the beginning — from the very first page I wrote — would elbow its way through to be heard, though I wasn't able, then, to pay it any mind. Like they say, the squeaky wheel gets the grease.

I have a friend whose taste in clothing is — what is the word? — dated. She is in her forties with a well-toned, athletic body. She rarely misses a workout. Yet she hasn't changed her hair style in two decades. And most of her clothes are the very ones she wore in college. I suspect her lack of style is on purpose. Here is where I should add that my friend has no financial difficulties. In fact, the opposite is true.

When we've met for lunch or dinner I've thought, *Oh. Doesn't she know how much older those clothes make her look? They are the clothes of someone who has no imagination, no confidence.*

I can't help it. Clothes are ... essential. Maybe not crucial. But significant. They lend a certain graciousness and say a lot about where someone has settled *internally*. I have to work really hard to keep my face from falling when I meet my friend. My feelings are usually so obvious, they might as well be a sign on my forehead.

The important thing is, five minutes into our conversation, our laughing, I don't give her clothes another thought. Okay, maybe one: *If she'd just ask me, I would share a few tidbits about keeping up with a certain personal style versus being trendy,* things along that nature. Nothing out of malice. Something that is both nice ... *and* true. I can do that.

I once worked as a professional personal shopper. I learned pretty quickly that when it comes to individual taste, it's best to remember that some women take delight in and will defend, like a dog with a fleshy bone, their preference of '70's peasant wear. Even when they are paying you plenty to overhaul it.

So while I don't relate to why my friend has such a blah-and-tactless wardrobe while she works so hard at staying fit and fresh otherwise, I do make an effort to appreciate a penchant for well-worn fashions through *her* eyes.

But it hasn't been easy for me. And I've failed in huge ways more than once. Consequently, I've been working through my conflicting feelings to get at the underlying truth of why someone else's style annoys me. I sensed there was more going on with me than the fact that I have two opposing personalities in regards to this issue: one is that I passionately love clothes and panache, the other is disliking how much I passionately love clothes and panache.

So I did a little research. Only to find what I believe is the real reason my friend's clothes bug me the way they do. And, as it turns out, it has little to do with her and all to do with my background and me. Which comes as no surprise.

I tell myself I'm not nostalgic for my heritage when I see this woman, that I am not looking at my family, my roots, that I know the difference between her life and my own. I tell myself this, but it's not true. She is the first Italian friend I've made since leaving the East Coast. And when I catch myself gauging her appearance, I wonder if I am any better than all those squinty-eyed, fault-finding European relatives I couldn't wait to leave behind.

Clothes conjure for me all the ethnicity of being Italian. After reading Maria Laurino's book, *Were You Always Italian?*, I came to see myself in relation to my background more clearly. Here's a passage that nearly undid me: *Italian culture means understanding a people that have, for centuries, felt the need to hide the impoverishment of their ancestry. To feast and dress well, to celebrate in spite of the fact there was little to go around is an attitude that has prevailed in Italian culture through the ages. Italians put their expectations for a better future into their clothes. They hold dear the romantic illusion that a beautiful, refined presentation can provide them with the essential self-confidence needed to compete in the world.*

This way of seeing things is as ingrained in me as my fingerprints and it pretty much defines my take on the world. I would never betray an Italian sense of good taste. So this is what bugs me, like it or not: How could my *Italian* friend dress like she does?

Could it be that because of some biologically deep-seated place, I can never reach past the fact that the way my friend dresses disrespects our shared heritage? Maybe I worked so hard at leaving some things about my past behind, that all the Italian-ness I thought I'd reinvented comes to the surface when I see my friend, sometimes in a surge that feels overpowering.

Okay, does that sound too far-fetched? Even if it makes some real sense to me?

It all seems so out of proportion to what is really important between friends. But I read once that a paradox is an important warning sign. *Is it?* I remember thinking.

I don't like admitting this: I tend to make swift judgements about the ultra-casual American way of dressing down, assessments that have often proved way off base. Especially when it comes to the larger issues of character and integrity. And, as I admit this, there's something about my *own* character that is causing the back of my neck to prickle.

What is beginning to really frighten me, though, especially since I now live in Seattle, home to comfy-frumpy, is that my Seattle friends will throw this book down, calling me a heartless snob, that this admission is going to annoy them right out of their Crocs.

Still, this was a complete and utter catharsis for me. And once I did the work of all that, I shared my breakthrough with my friend. Talk about honesty. Boy did we have a laugh, the best laughing jag, the kind that comes from the gut when you aren't pretending.

So why was I honest with her? You must be asking yourself this. Because I also knew she's known all along how I feel. And this conversation was good for our friendship. Sometimes humor is the best equalizer. It can lighten the climate between friends, oh, at least a ton.

Unless it totally flops. (Life is a risk.)

I told my friend that when we are old women, she will be the one whose bank account still shines and I'll be the one with a mountain of shoes stacked in a rusty grocery cart.

"I'll take you in," she said.

Again, we laughed. I remember trembling inside, out of appreciation and a deep sense of respect for my friend. My favorite combination.

I can tell you a story. My friend has the worst manners in a restaurant. She's never had to work as a waitress. When we go out to eat, she treats the waiter like domestic help. It's embarrassing.

The woman talking here is a hair dresser. Maybe thirty years old. She combs out my wet hair as she talks. I don't consciously set out to ask *every*one I talk to about friendship. But most of the time I can't help it. Plus, she is, as I said, combing my hair. We get to talking. This book is so nosey.

We've been friends since college. She was the debutante and I was on student loans. We clicked. I was going to talk to her about the way she acts when we go out to eat. But I figure no one is perfect.. Usually I make some excuse and run back to put another five dollar bill on the table. It's my way of apologizing to the waitress.

In the time it takes to find and plug in a flat iron, this woman taught me so much. Sometimes the simplest act is the strongest gesture.

I'm sitting in my office, nursing a second cup of coffee and trying to come to grips with the fact that, contrary to every-thing I'm saying here, writing a book about friendship allows me a lot less time to take part in it. I have invitations I haven't responded to, emails I haven't answered, a dear friend who has become a mother since I went to work on the final drafts, and I haven't been to visit her and baby Hannah yet (Will you ever forgive me, Jenn?). I take a sip and start in on the closing paragraphs for this chapter:

What I'm about to say is not a novel insight, it's just one I haven't mentioned yet and I think it's time to: How I feel about *myself* in another's company is the litmus test. If I can be myself, honest in a way that lets me feel good about myself, then I bask in the friendship and will gladly do the work of maintaining it. And it *is* work. Good, hard work. People forget this sometimes.

I think friendship really has less to do with the other person, and more to do with the question: Do I like *myself* while I'm with her/him? If the answer is yes, I think the question of how honest we are with each other will work itself out over the years, in the ways that matter.

Last week, I visited my eighty-six-year-old friend, Elizabeth. I love how she makes me feel about aging. She skims off the fear I have of it, and renders it back to me in ways that remind me that, in fact, creases and lines make us more real: without them, guidance, the guidance I *need,* would vanish. She helps me see how far I've come. Who I am now. Who I will become. She's the wise woman and I am the grateful student, if not my only mentor, surely my favorite. I don't have this kind of relationship with my own mother so I've always been out there looking for it. My own mother is a wise-woman too, but the very nature of mother-daughter makes for more of a push-pull, more of a concession.

Here's what Elizabeth said to me:

Between people, honesty is, or it isn't! Knowing when it's right to be straight with someone is a lesson hard learned. Because if any part of the brain the good Lord gave you doubts you should be honest, and you mouth off just the same, Honey, that is not honesty. That's ego!

It was, without a doubt, the shrewdest advice I've ever

received. It burrowed in. And I quickly found myself in a place where all of my friendship examining could never take me, a place past all the complicated emotions, to where one can only come to with age.

And whether the idea of getting to a place where you can finally know, own, and say exactly where you stand on life's issues without apology comforts you, I really can't say.

But right now I have the urge to stand up and shout, *HALL-E-LU-JAH! Hallelujah, hallelujah.*

So I know it comforts me.

NAMING THE BIRD — *for Jackie*

I'm grateful for my new friend
who says *grosbeak*
as one flies through an awning of poplars so tall
we stroll under a canopy of shade. I'm here
in the Northwest twenty years
and still know only the ordinary
crow, robin, wren.

She and I leave this place behind
in mind. What we think takes root and grows huge
into small talk: politics, marriage, men
with ponytails hanging gray. *How weary they look*
gone to seed like that.

I've missed this kind of intensity
meant not to separate but stimulate
for the sake of it.

How easy it is to startle the locals, we say,
with our frank ways and words
without even trying. I tell her last time I tried,
really tried
was at a conference on the waterfront
where I sat with a name tag, pinned
between two men, one using the word *cunt*
two, three times in reference to his ex-wife,
bringing back a side of me I'd nearly silenced
since moving to Seattle.

What I did was pour my wine
into his crotch, splashing through hesitation
I would have made a pact with if I'd paused

to censor myself,
stopping short of doing
what needed doing.

THREE

How Could You?

*"We shelter children for a time; and that is all.
We owe them nothing, and are owed nothing. I think we
owe our friends more, especially our female friends."*

—FAY WELDON

I t's an early grey morning in September. And windy. Rain
strikes the skylight. I don't want to get up so I lie here
thinking about this next, potentially grim, chapter. All week
I've been hoping I'd think of an opening line to point the way
into this. So far, nothing. "This is bad." I tell my husband.

"Not so bad," he says. "You just need to slow boil it like
an egg. Don't try and roast the whole chicken."

This makes me laugh, and not just because I want to
laugh. It sure beats going to work. It makes me laugh because
Larry has been watching The Food Network.

"Quoting Rachael Ray again?" I say.

He smiles and nods his head.

"You have a crush on her."

He hesitates. He laughs. He shakes his head.

"Do you know how red your face gets when you lie?"

I am surprised by how fast he leaves the room. Rachael

would let him eat more meat, for one thing.

I love how Larry can say what is — even when he borrows from Rachel — just *how* it is. No fussy description. The simplicity is something I can turn to, something to depend on. Have I ever had a friendship as deeply connected and generous as my marriage? Honestly? Almost. But not quite.

So why am I teary?

Because I know how lucky I am.

And tears come easily when I'm needy. As needs go, I think I have a real one in front of me. I need to find a way to tell my mother's story without every bit of my past backing up on me. My parents' divorce is an old injury. I want to clean out the wound without reliving all the hurt. It's a messy account of friendship, a humbling story of losing faith and crawling back.

I don't miss all that.

Plus, sometimes I feel too old to talk about my parents. Other times, too young. I don't yet know all the ways their lives have impacted my own.

So I'm going to mention a few other stories first, okay? Just to prepare myself. Then I'll get to mom and dad. Without saying too much or being too vague. Too much would be excruciating. Too little and I'd have to question why I was telling it in the first place. Mostly, I fear it's one of those stories when the truth does more damage than good. Because the truth is just like the past, isn't it? It depends entirely on who's remembering it.

It's no accident Larry chose the "slow boil" comment to help me get started this morning. I told him how tentatively the following stories were disclosed to me. Not because the women I talked to didn't want to share their feelings, they did. It's just that little stands between them and the deceit they went through but pain. The mere mention of the word *betrayal* seems to evoke so much emotion that one woman, ten minutes into our talk, decided not to go over her story with me after all. "I have to tell you, I'm not sure I can do this. I'm sorry," she said wearily, and a bit watery-eyed. Sometimes, when I'm confronted with this anguish all over again, I wonder how my mother managed to put together a new life at all.

"Don't be," I said. Then we sat there for a while, each wishing the other would decide to tell her story. Or maybe I was projecting, and I was the only one wishing that. Maybe she was wishing I'd change the subject.

Another was so charged recounting the betrayal she experienced that I was unable to jot her story down with any coherency. She was adrenaline in high heels, cursing and name-calling. All of it hid more than it revealed, of course, but she was too young for me to point it out. I didn't want to risk sounding patronizing. It can be tough to get the tone right with twenty-somethings. I'm still not exactly sure what happened. She described vehemently what went down, giving me something of a rough summary. Someone's ex-wife was sleeping with her lover (or her ex-lover?) or *some*one's ex-somebody — Jeeze, I still don't know. Then she sort of stormed off. And that was fine with me.

What did I learn? First, that when I talk to others about feeling betrayed, I feel less anxious. The fact that it can sometimes feel like there is little conscience out there scares me less if I find someone willing to drop her guard and not pretend the experience was any easier than it was.

A practicing therapist told me that when she felt betrayed by a woman she thought was her friend, nothing really helped. Therapy certainly didn't, she admitted. Friends didn't. Drugs? Maybe. Then she laughed from deep in her belly. I took that as a good sign. "There is no other hurt like it. Believe me," she said. "Time restored me. And planning my revenge!" But humor had trickled in. Perspective. Maybe she wouldn't need to remove her ex-friend's fingernails with pliers after all. "Watch out for friends who pay your husband too much attention, you know the type."

I do.

Secondly, that there is no easy way to shake off hurt. You just get past it, eventually, hopefully.

Plus, I'm convinced the word *betrayal* has more definitions than I ever thought. My heart was in my throat when I started going over my notes. Apparently, we can betray someone by doing too much or by doing nothing. By speaking out or by keeping quiet. We can betray a friend by not finding the time to let her confide in us at all. I bet most of us have at one time or another.

Man, that's a lot to think about! Which is what I said to Larry after I read him that last paragraph.

"Let's go out for Thai food," he answered.

Oh, twist my arm.

My mother's story — I want to tell it because I not only promised her I'd include it, but I promised myself. Like I said, I could be making a mistake, but I'm used to that. So here it is:

My mother relied on a particular friend for companionship for nearly half of the twenty-five years she was married to my uncommunicative father. This friend was so trusted and familiar in our home that my sisters and I referred to her as "Auntie."

You've guessed what happens next, right? I remember that time in my family life and my chest feels constricted again in the same way it did then. I wonder whether I will ever be free of this feeling. I'm sure my mother won't.

Every woman knows the ultimate betrayal one woman can bestow on another is to pretend to be her friend's confidant while, simultaneously, plotting to steal her husband away.

Once the theft was obvious, a divorce (a messy, painful, melodramatic divorce) between my parents ensued. And my father later (actually, pretty quickly) married my mother's "best" friend.

But here's what I find most amazing: A year after the divorce my mother admitted that she felt a deeper level of betrayal from her friend then from my father. In fact, she went so far as to say she missed her friend and the intimacy they once shared more than she missed her marriage. Her admission planted the first seed for this chapter.

I keyed right into the word my friend, Michael, used to describe a friend capable of this kind of deceit: *frenemy*. He said the word has been around for ages. "Where have you *been*, girlfriend?" But it was the first time I heard the word and — wow — right after he said it, I felt like it was unleashed into the world just for my mother.

Frankly, I don't know how my mother learned to trust again. The very two people she counted on to stand by her through life's turns betrayed her. Together! Yet, somehow she found the courage to find the beginning of herself all over again. But she will never completely forgive them. Nor will I. That would be too much to dress up and pretend.

The one time I tuned into Dr. Phil to see what all the fuss was about, he said, "For every toxic person or experience we encounter, there's an equal positive force available to us." Force? Hooey. I dismissed it as self-help babble. I think things are more random and that we can't direct our lives to the nth degree no matter what we say to ourselves over and over.

At the same time, his words struck a chord and I began to realize the real stuff of his message: Recently an optimistic, supportive friend came into my life subsequent to my finally letting go of a friendship I was maintaining out of some worn sense of obligation. I had long-past ceased to find any pleasure in it.

Then I watched this same "force" open to my mother in a more fundamental way. After anger and agonizing took long, sharp bites out of her self-esteem for nearly three years, she finally found the resilience to step outside herself and move away (emotionally as well as geographically) from the "toxicity." Once she did, a new life more to her liking presented itself in ways she hadn't expected.

The move took courage. By definition, courage is not the absence of fear or despair, but the strength to move forward in spite of them. And it's a wonderful thing to witness from a daughter's perspective. As my mother found the courage within, she threw me a life-line. I wonder if mothers fully realize how closely their daughters watch for this kind of knowledge. Now, when I doubt my own nerve, I think of this time in her life.

I also learned that courage, however manifested, is what it takes to move past the hopelessness that sets in when you've been betrayed by someone you love. You simply have to rise each day regardless of the desire to entomb yourself in blankets, put one foot in front of the other, and carry on no matter what. Supportive friends help a lot. But no one can do the work for you. I knew my mother felt truly alone for the first time in her life and it really scared her.

I tried sharing with her what I've practiced in my own life as a writer, alone in my office most of every day. And what I've learned by talking with my circle of friends, women who don't mind sharing what goes on with them: that only by facing our aloneness do we become the women we need to. I don't think I need a PhD to say that.

But this is such new, awkward territory for my mother. And most of the time any advice from me gets lost somewhere between us, in a place where there's nothing but the two of us trying to avoid each other's eyes. She doesn't come from a generation of unorthodox women. Typical of post-war times when she was newly married, and after my father made enough money, we moved from our inner-city neighborhood to suburbia where my mother became an isolated mother of three in a split-level home at the end of a Connecticut cul-de-sac. Bigger home. Smaller life.

Still, it never occurred to her to object to leaving her friends, family, and neighborhood behind. And my father offered little by way of companionship. He was a provider not a conversational intimate. Sometimes we forget we are the first generation in which men are expected to work at being in touch with the emotional lives of their wives and children. Or their *own*, for that matter. I think men talk about sports because they store their emotions under layers and layers until there is no storage space left. Then they blow. Or play golf.

I like to think of my mother's empowerment like child-birth. Even if you haven't read a thousand instructional books on the subject, you will squat and push when you need to. Will and instinct kick in. I've seen this enough to say it (and remembering it may be the numero uno reason I've never had a baby). I've craned my neck and squinted and grimaced at three home births and two hospital births and I'm all set, thank God, to say "no thank you" when and if I'm asked to do so again.

My mother found a new definition of fulfillment during the next phase of her life when she was living alone in California without the complications of marriage. It was the first time she could do only for herself, away from obligations, duty, meal schedules. I enjoyed watching her polish her new life, like silver under her own attention.

Being forced to drift off-course, my mother had no choice but to find her way back. Still, I think women of my mother's generation have a hard time admitting they like living alone. As if saying so makes them selfish or self-centered.

They were raised to be care-givers. But caretakers often neglect themselves. I watched my mother blossom during this independent time in her life and I discovered something else. We are much more alike than I'd ever imagined.

This woman and I communicated by email. I met her on an airplane. After I stoked my seat mate into a speedy conversation about friendship, disloyalty, and the many thoughts my questions stirred up in her, she promised to send me an email describing something she experienced at work. She said she didn't want to discuss it midair. She was on her way to a business meeting and talking any more about betrayal would turn her much-needed bravado into mush.

I sat there thinking about how we all struggle to keep up a brave front. But facing a boardroom has got to take the cake.

Airplanes have a humbling effect on me. I feel vulnerable as the plane plows on, my nerves coming undone one synapse at a time. I'm always thinking "what if this is my last conversation?" The calm woman beside me was my perfect seat mate. As our plane trembled through the belly of a squall, she seemed so poised and positive.

So not like me, I thought. Me? I ordered another teeny-tiny bottle of vodka.

As promised, here's my story. I'm a little embarrassed. It reads like a B-Rated movie.

Back then, the plan was to leave my position and start my own advertising agency. I shared my plans with only one colleague. I thought she and I were friends. I'm afraid not.

Anyway, I needed a year, maybe two, before I could afford to move on.

Then one night I saw my friend and my boss leaving a bar together. So many things started to add up. The way she would defend him all the time. Even the way she was dressing differently. I got it! Our boss was a control-freak. She and I used to joke about that. He was picking out her clothes. I started going over everything I had divulged. I began to panic.

The next day I confronted her. All she said was her loyalty was to the agency. I couldn't believe what bullshit I was hearing. Soon after, I was ostracized by my co-workers because I was no longer part of the team. Those last months were hell.

I know you probably want to know why I didn't quit sooner. I needed the money. Part of my plan included saving more money. I stuck it out.

The worst part? My so-called friend disposed of our friendship and felt no regret. Any dealings we had were clipped and tense. I tried to pretend that work meant nothing more to me than what I was being paid for. The upshot was I learned what I could handle.

Now I'm very strict about keeping my professional and my personal relationships separate. I don't talk about my personal life at work. There is one woman I hired that I really like. She has this quirky sense of humor that helps us all get through the pressure cooker our work is. I'm tempted to initiate a friendship outside the office because I enjoy her so much. So far I haven't. I'm leery of friendship in a way I never wanted to be. I can't trust myself to trust her.

But I have so little time outside of work to meet other women. I feel pretty lonely for a friend who knows me.

I was reading an email but I swear it sounded as if her voice just drifted off.

I shot back, "Ask the woman in your office out for a drink. Trust again. Please? For both of us."

About an hour went by. Her reply was, *Okay. I will. I need the feeling of possibility in this area of my life again.*

I thought that's what people say when they mean it.

Ever since our exchange I've been asking myself: Am I too

used to disposable things? If I fling things away simply because I have the financial means to, does this affect how I care for my relationships? Am I loyal enough? I'm beginning to wonder.

Here is where I get touchy about the word *loyalty,* eager to move forward as I usually am.

For starters, I'm a hairdresser-hopper. That's not very loyal. And I prefer my friends to my family most of the time.

These questions are saddling my mind. I'm a little huffy. Last night I told Larry that I'm sick to death of cleaning the house, ironing his shirts, *cooking!*

"I iron my own shirts and do most of the cooking," he reminded me.

I rubbed my forehead. "I think I'm afraid that all *this,*" I pointed at my computer screen, "will demand too much of me. That's the problem. I don't think I can improve *enough.*"

"My God," he said, and he put his arms around my back, hugging me as if he could protect me from something. What a tranquilizer his front cupping my back is for me. "Give yourself a break."

I agreed to try. And to turn off my computer right then. What a guy.

Re-reading my mother's story, makes me feel a little lean, emotionally.

But then the words, *Okay. I will. I need the feeling of possibility in this area of my life again* jump off the page and I'm grinning again. An equal mix. Just the kind of balance I was looking for.

A MARRIAGE — *for M.*

Fifteen minutes into my morning routine
the phone rings.

Outside, spring swells
warm from the earth, the first sprouting
which brings to mind moments of pure joy
I once felt tending the soil so gloriously rich,
awe spread through me like a current.

But, like years, wants move on
by winding down the way lust abates
or snaring like tissue caught in barbed-wire.

Now, with so much to weed, I'd rather write.
I can't neglect the query life is.
So I neglect the garden.

It's a friend (a friend I have misgivings about)
calling to say her man left her
for a tango dancer with long red hair
and breasts borne of silicone.

As if a slap bores through the cable
connecting us, I put my hand to my cheek,
my own loyal marriage unable to console.

When she arrives, her eyes are red
as the lipstick I wear. I've never known her like this.
Normally, we're not this candid.

Funny (funny as in *strange*), don't you think,
that betrayal is our first setting for trust?

She tries to rationalize the deceit,
leans her body into mine as if our touch is a bond
that bears up.

Oh *no*.
My husband's tears turn the room to half-mast.

I bypass this moist emotion,
head straight for anger.
Not rage. Not a child yelling
I hate you I hate you I hate you
but wrath that is courage of another kind.
Like blurting. Or telling the truth.
There isn't enough of it these days.

Instead, we hush ourselves, pretend,
call it something else.

FOUR

Notes on a Metamorphosis

*"There are people who take the heart out of you,
and there are people who put it back."*

—ELIZABETH DAVID

A year ago, if you had asked me, I would have said that I likely wouldn't write the story I'm about to tell. I'd talk about it, definitely, but I had come to believe talking is sometimes enough. Not every idea has to flow through my fingertips onto the page. I didn't find this restrictive; I found it incredibly freeing. My desire for good conversation — or silence — is finally on a par with my desire to write.

Telling it sort of comes to my rescue, though, and quashes my first thought that was: *I just worry that you're going to sound a little crazy here.*

Not that I know from experience, my next thought shot back, *but the world* is *crazy.*

It feels good to finally admit that for nearly two decades (mid twenties to mid forties) I kept bumping up against the same wall with friends. Three friends, that is, in immediate succession. Each raised a lot of questions for me about the kind of women I was befriending and what it takes to turn an acquaintance into a friend, a friend into a close friend, and why we either continue as friends or let the friendship go. In each of these, we let it go. But, dammit, why?

Maybe it's just the nature of relationships, with all their puzzling changeability. But I don't think I can let myself off the hook that easily. My best guess is that, over and over, I chose the same woman in a different body: A head-turning, beautiful blonde (with breasts!). An all-American-W.A.S.P. sprung from the Midwest with an upper-middle-class background, and everything a short, dark, flat-chested, kinky-haired, East Coast, Catholic-born, daughter of a working class Italian immigrant, me, was not. And each possessed a beguiling charisma I repeatedly confused with confidence. What a relief it was to finally see beyond my hurt and discover I was at fault for the break up of these friendships. Gulp. But, not so fast. As it turns out, it wasn't because of something I did or said. At least, not intentionally.

I promise to get back to all this, return to these three women the way actors do in a call back. But this other thought is being really pushy right now: In my thirties, finding a "best" friend, was still the point of my search. I hadn't yet stretched to that other side of friendship, the side where I didn't give over so much, didn't *expect* so much. I wonder sometimes if I didn't go about my friendships with my arms held out as if to embrace my friend's wants while forgetting to pay close enough attention to my own. So like a woman. So like me. Then.

"Your best friend search is really a search for your mother," my new late-night, beer-drinking chum said, a woman I met while in residence at an artist colony in Costa Rica. She and I swapped friendship stories one moon-bright, tropical night. Residencies are intimacy-speed balls, part work-intensive, part dorm-life, artists and writers in temporary flight from the day-to-day, engaging in close-knit conversations with others who are also a long way from home and a little lonely by now.

They are also kind of exhausting, living and working like that.

There we were, two women in our forties, eating popcorn and guzzling Coronas at mid-night, free of domestic responsibilities that swallow up huge chunks of our time back home. If up this late in Seattle, I'd be folding laundry or emptying the dishwasher, trying to stay ahead of the next chore that always needs doing. It was fantastic to feel a lack of obligation to anything other than writing.

I listened intently as she told me about her therapy back home in California (who isn't in therapy back home in California?) because she'd recently "broken up" with her best friend. "My therapist said that women can make the mistake of trying to recreate the intimacy they once had with their mothers or *wished* they'd had with their mothers. They look for mother-close intimacy with women friends. But it's an intimacy that can't be replicated. We'll always be disappointed unless we modify our expectations," she warned. "Especially if your mom let you down. Then it's easy to want way too much from friendship."

I just stared at her for a minute, my mouth an open oval. "Is it really that simple?" I finally asked, my mind all aflutter. I felt like she was on to something, something that might unlock some of my confusion, that her words were some new key. "I mean are we really trying to recreate how secure it felt to hold our mother's hand? A love exclusive as that!?"

"Yes, I think so," she said, "that's how needy we are."

"MYGOD!" I yelled as if I'd just found another cockroach the size of my thumb, "I've been looking for my mother? I thought I was trying to get *away* from my mother." Mind you, I was well into my third cerveza by then.

"Ditto here," she said. "But think more in terms of a fairy *god*mother."

I sensed she was exactly right.

Sitting there under a ceiling fan, floppy leaves of a banana tree patting my screen door, I honestly felt like something old shook off me. I'd simply been in want of too much. I didn't even bother to write anything down. I just sat there feeling it. It was powerful. And it was enough.

Was it because my mother and I have always had a bumpy relationship? Was I seeking from my friends a smoother ride? Why had I not made this connection before?

God I'm a late bloomer.

That night I couldn't turn off my mind. I lie awake replaying our conversation. Why *was* I so thrown? I'd already learned a similar truth about marriage, sometimes the loneliest relationship of all once we discover that love is *not* enough. Imagine my surprise when, at the naive age of barely-twenty-one, I learned one person is never enough for another. And though I am one of the fortunate ones, blessed with a marriage that grew with and not against me, still, as a young woman I was unprepared for how much work it was to maintain, how much it takes to ensure the relationship doesn't bottleneck but stretches over time. My work became, at every turn, figuring out which gaps to slide into alone, which we needed to dive into together, and which to jump over. I wasn't nuts for all this problem solving, either. I was crazy in love with my husband, though. That helps. He has a character that is rooted in honesty, even if I have to remind him (constantly) to share his thoughts with me. "Oh, what's the use trying to talk about this?" I have said a zillion times. "You don't even know how you *feel* about it, so how can you talk about it?" I think most women can relate.

To finally understand my search for a best friend was about wanting an exclusivity — a mother-safety-net — made a lot of sense to me. Perhaps I thought the perfect friend would help bring me up all over again.

Then I thought: If the very definition of exclusivity means individual, separate, single, sole, was this friendship journey simply about being mother and friend to myself? If so, how *cliche*.

So now what?

I know how tedious it is to say a woman needs to be her own best friend, how repetitious it sounds. Still, when insight comes to me as one of those pushy 3 a.m. confrontations when all doubts seem to gather en masse and demand I think instead of sleep, I take note. Funny thing, I woke up relieved. *Let's try this*, I told myself, *let's go with this whole self-as-best-friend-cliche-thing*. I thought this time an answer had finally come down from the sky. And because I was in need of something to open up my suspicions about everything that was wrong with my current pattern of friendships, I latched on for dear life.

Emotionally, though, I was still in the habit of eagerness, only beginning to grasp the changes I needed to make in order to stroll my way more s-l-o-w-l-y through a friendship so that it didn't run its course and peter out as quickly as it had come. Even so, the breakthrough helped me ease up. Enough so I could begin to welcome instead of fear the confusion I felt.

And, as the story usually goes, that's when this other truth popped into focus: Since I was a kid, I've craved alone-ness. Even then, silence felt like the greatest luxury. Who knows why it took me so long to say this. Maybe I was afraid of the implications: that if I enjoyed aloneness *too* much, I would end up alone. Oh, the fears we entertain before we learn to trust ourselves.

But what about the collective message that *together* equals the right way to live and *alone* equals the sad alternative? How many times have I entered a restaurant, eager for a good meal, my own company, and a little variance from my routine of eating, say, a hard boiled egg over the sink (Larry travels a lot and so do I), only to have the experience ruined as the hostess asks, "Just you?" Then, as soon as I'm seated someone rushes over to remove the second table setting as if I'd not just filled a space but vacated half of it. *"Oh, for christ's sake!"* I think because nothing is going to stand in this waiter's way of removing the silverware, plate and glass, least of all courtesy.

This too: After, say, an hour tops, I feel unnerved around groups of people. The slow pace of group decisions and the small talk makes me feel like I'm stuck in first gear. I can feel myself revving, but there is no where to go with my rpm. After a dose of it, aloneness lets me feel like I'm moving again. "Maybe it's just an Italian thing," I said to Larry once. "No, it's you," he said. Oh, what does he know.

Still, the ease that made its way in that long sleepless night restored me in so many ways. I still think about lying there deep in a foreign jungle listening to myself molt, fears busting free. Ever since, I've been able to accept my friendship flubs and flaws with humor. And if a friendship doesn't pan out it's not as much of a heart break. It's a relief to finally be able to say, "Yeah, I screwed up. I gave too much, expected too little. Whatever. Next?" After years of false starts and relapses, it's the perfect gift to myself.

"Why *is* granting ourselves forgiveness so much harder than forgiving others?" I asked my friend back at the artist colony. She thinks guilt works something like a safety valve for society. "Forgiving others makes us feel good about ourselves," she said. "But if we were to forgive ourselves too easily we wouldn't develop a strong enough moral sense. We'd be living in a world of sociopaths. Would you prefer that?"

I guess not.

"What about the Catholics and their confessions?" I asked, more to prod her than anything. I already knew what she was going to say.

"Why do you think those blood-thirsty, boy-fucking old men came up with that ridiculous idea in the first place? How convenient." We laughed so hard. I was just so in heaven.

Back to the point. Once I finally whacked my leanings toward self-blame upside the head and felt them slither to the ground, I thought *This is it, the combined result of all this work!* And I'm not about to let them squeeze back in and spoil things. I've grown to love how I can make my way through the maze of getting to know someone, without the same level of expectation or letdown. I finally get how uncomfortable it's all supposed to feel — change, friendship, *life*. Not always, certainly. But pretty much.

I'm pretty sure I began wanting people (everyone) to like me at a very young age. This is the stuff I never talk about with anyone, but I think my father's lack of interest in a third daughter when he longed for a son didn't make me love him any less. It spurred me on. I spent a lot of time and emotional energy trying to get him to notice me. *Oh, no*, I hear myself say as I dip into the past again. *Oh, shush! There are always the little fall-backs, the little wounds that still need healing.*

Maybe every friendship of mine is measured against this want, this longing for a safe haven, a home. *Oh, no*, I hear myself again. This time at three times the volume. Now I wonder if I've also been on a "father-net" search. This thought splashes all over me. Sorry but I'm temporarily lost in a wave.

There. Now I can go on.

Whoa! High tide. A lot of debris to wade through.

This is what floats to the top: Now that I'm aware that,

from a young age, I've had to be both mother and father to myself, emotionally, where did this lead me to?

Easy. Into becoming a writer.

I look up from my screen, stunned. Man, how many thoughts showed up today. And all at once.

It's probably a good idea to streamline again, to get back to my original "metamorphosis" which is, in a nutshell, this: I developed a puzzling aversion to the very two words I thought I needed most: *best friend.* Funny how that goes. Strung together, they sounded so schoolgirl, so dependent. I wanted another idiom. One more grown-up because I saw myself differently. I'd turned a page. Even "girlfriend" didn't sound right and I felt silly saying it. Perhaps there was no word. Other than just "friend." Yes. *Friend* is the word for what I feel, I told myself, it holds enough weight.

And I began to speculate how good it would feel to enter a new friendship with a stronger self at the helm. If I couldn't find new friendships through "dating" to sustain me during this next phase of my life, I would have to face more aloneness than I'd bargained for. What scared me most was that there would be just the same old me all over again.

But I have a confession to make: At the time of this writing, my connections to all of my friendships seem more on track, more fulfilling than ever. (Thank you, Jeane. Thank you, Sheila, Thank you, Amagit, Libby, Joy, Jackie, and Diane.)

And my new-friendship search is going better than I imagined. Of course, I still have downfalls, a few more bad dates than related to you in Chapter One. Such as: dinner with one woman who kept stuffing the butter and jam packets in her purse, another with a woman who drank three cocktails as I nursed one and got so drunk I had to ask the waiter to call her a cab.

Then there was the woman who lived in my building who rushed into my life with what seemed like a trust-able thread for a connection, and before I could even remember her last name, she disappeared. Poof!

Still, I kept rallying my courage. And, low and behold, two women I invited out, one for lunch, another for dinner, have become dear and trusted friends. And when we talk about friendship, it seems we've all found the same answer: that intimacy is something we hold inside ourselves, that it involves separateness as much as togetherness. And isn't possible if one comes without the other. One of them said this: *Finding a good fit between people is something we can't do at all. It's something that happens. You can't push it.*

Her words give me even more resilience by my relating them to you.

Okay, The Callback, as promised!

I don't think it necessary to go into the individual details of my failed-friendship-triad, the one I set this chapter into motion with before I detoured like crazy. I'm more interested in the similarities not only in these three women's qualities, but in my reactions to them.

I'll begin by saying how much it amazed me to find that, each time, the woman I thought was my closest friend was doing little to perk up my joy in life. Even as I began to change my ideas of what constituted a satisfying friendship, I still remember feeling an annoying thing in their company:

a willingness to compromise myself in ways I believed would hold our friendship in place. And just kind of ignoring it. Like the top shelf of a closet that won't sort itself. And trying to hang on to a friend when you sense a real moving apart is like trying to cling to youth. I can exercise, take a myriad of vitamins, eat my salmon and soy but, even so, youthfulness slips away. These days, I already look more like my mother than myself.

Which dismays in all the usual ways.

And is the same scary lesson I needed to learn about friendship.

Where to begin?

Especially when saying what I'm about to reveal feels so private and embarrassing that telling it is like swigging Scotch right from the bottle. Just thinking about it makes my eyes water, my face flush.

Looking back, it seems too simplistic to say I fell for these women. It was more like a bad case of *there's a big part of me that wants to be you*. I was afraid to admit this never mind write about it. But I lived with the feeling. Way past the moment I knew it was high time to do something about it. What silly, untrue ideas had skewed my confidence so?

Then I read an article referring to these as "Girl Crushes." I felt a rush of gratitude for such a no-nonsense description of something I felt but couldn't put a name to. Or nail down its effect on me. I didn't discuss this with anyone but was pretty sure it was a fingerprint. I now had a clue, a starting place.

To paraphrase what I learned in this illuminating article by Caroline Knapp: These crushes can be tremendously instructive because they help us shed light on some of our wants for ourselves. We are attracted to these kinds of friendships because we feel the women have attributes we desire and are based on admiration. And how the crush usually subsides once we really get to know our friend, flaws and all.

Not only did I like reading that, I believed it. And it made me think how much of life is always about learning from those we look up to, from infancy to maturity. Which made me think about how many kinds of love there are.

To be honest, more than beauty (though I wanted more of that, too), I wanted what I perceived as confidence. Blonde physical beauty still translated into "having it all" to me and I hadn't even begun to understand how much of an act social charm (a little too slick with an ability to turn on the charisma) can be. I did not even dream how much insecurity it can cover up.

And yet, unlike something I admired, each was willing to settle, repeatedly, for financial and love lives turbulent as our Northwest skies in winter. I couldn't yet read the warning signs of what this says about their ability to be a sustaining friend. But I was beginning to see *some*thing was amiss.

"Do you think it's true, that we can have sort of a crush on our friends at first?" I asked Larry, all chit-chatty because I didn't want my question to seem like the big fat deal it felt like. I was afraid that if I made too much a deal out of it, I might ... make too much a deal out of it. I was amazed how calm my voice came out. Even though my question wasn't so much about friendship but a kind of desperation. There is no avoiding saying that.

After a long moment of silence he said, "W-w-what? I dunno. What do you mean by crush?"

"I'm not sure." And I wasn't.

"Should I be worried?"

I smirked.

"Ask Oprah."

What baffles me is why I asked Larry in the first place. So I asked Suze Orman. Well, not really, but I read her column faithfully (for awhile) and in one of them she addressed the whole issue of unreliable friends. Which isn't the whole "crush" topic, per se, but it helped me define some things that my own experience wasn't able to reach. According to Suze, traits like cheating on spouses and bad credit debt can make people unreliable friends because "in the end, it's all about responsibility."

I think I made a rather loud exhalation noise after reading that. And this thought promptly filled my head: *Take your heart and run!* Maybe I drew these women to me because, just as the saying goes, what we fear most, we draw. Unbeknownst to me (at least consciously) at the time, I chose women who extended my lack of self-confidence. And once I got below the surface of their impeccable facades, what I found was startling: these women had less self-confidence than I did! How about that.

Is it in the Chinese language where the word "crisis" has the same meaning as the word "opportunity?" Because when I finally walked away from one of these friendships, or felt the profound hurt as another walked away from me, a crises did ensue, an utter loss of self as another painful search for intimacy went awry. I felt tired, frustrated, depressed. I passed from weariness to anger to indifference. Only finally circling in on a term I'd heard repeatedly over the years but never applied to my own hang-ups: co-dependency. *Sheesh! Another cliche.* That old hyphenated word is so done, so passé, so over. But apparently I'd still mistaken it for friendship.

Frumpish, foolish me.

The realization was daunting. And, yet, with another breath I clung to these friendships. I still believed that friendship, even when it no longer satisfied, was the yarn holding me together. I had little faith that I would be okay if I trusted the voice of Wiser-Older-Woman who, by then, sat squarely on my shoulder shouting, "You wouldn't need to cling if this woman was your *friend*."

I sensed she was the only cord I could hold onto until the rest of me caught up. And gradually, once I began to trust her over the voice of the other mean and shameless woman who hovers in the background, Miss Fear-Of-Everything, I had a new way to deal with my friendships. And it made for its own mood. My new language was braver. I felt a new certainty. Most of the time, anyway. Definitely *some* of the time.

It was as if the very definition of friendship I was looking for took shape. My need of it did not become something less in my life, but it did become something less desperate.

When I read over this chapter, I can feel, in fast-forward, my "metamorphosis" all over again. And how everything began to fall into place once I began to focus on what I wanted from friendship instead of what I feared I could lose. It freed me up.

Which brings me to the most incredible acknowledgment a woman (at least *this* woman) can bask in. Ta-da! I realize it was me all along who held the qualities I most wanted to possess.

Little ole me.

I am a bit overcome.

THE ACTRESS — *for Bonnie*

The way you looked up
from the dryer as I came in the door,
your arms full of clothes, *hi*
formed with your mouth
but no sound

the way you dropped your bundle
and took me by the hand

the way you led me to your yard
sunk deep in summer bloom, branching
all angles to the light

the way your kid's tree fort came into view
as more than a clumsy mix of wood and nails
and made me long
to pull myself up by its laddered mane.

I would like to say I came for solace
but, truth is, I didn't.
It's just that soon as I see you,
if any little thing struggles internal,
my guard tumbles down

and from my eyes
whole rivers spill
until laughter lightens me
as we talk on, and on, and on
nodding yes, and no, and yes, a gust of giving
we ride like gulls.

How healing to lie back into what I've needed
all my life to know, trust
warm as a newly ironed shirt.

Perhaps others have known it, felt it
when you're the lead on stage
or in a minor role when motherhood and marriage fray
the edges of your life.

Regardless
we fall under your enormous spell
as a light opens for us
and we open to let it in.

FIVE

Max & Me
and Baby Makes Three

*"Good communication with a friend, especially when
differences arise, is as stimulating as black coffee,
and just as hard to sleep after."*

— ANNE MORROW LINDBERGH

The other day, while riding the city bus, I related parts of this next story to a complete stranger. Lately, it's been circling in the back of my mind whenever I see a mother and child on the street. And last night, I talked to my friend Max on the phone and I thought, *okay, it's time to get this story onto the page.* Such moments of clarity about what to write about and what to leave in mind go through me like a sewing needle lately, partly because they are so rare.

Here it is, then, Max and me, boiled down to a few pages of togetherness: Years back, when my friend, Max, broke the news to me that she was pregnant, instead of feeling happy for her, I immediately felt something akin to betrayal. Ah, Jesus, I thought, as my face flushed red and there was this strange tightening in my stomach, a knot twining all by itself. After a heavy silence, I forced a big fake smile onto my face. I'm sure I looked like one of those dolls that spring from a colorful metal box, bounding up from the table with an ear-to-ear grin and arms wide open.

Why couldn't I just be happy for her? That would take me some time to figure out. I willed myself to feel happy for her. *I'm really happy for her*, I thought, *of course I am*. But waves of panic shivered through me and there was a huge part of me that feared our friendship was as doomed as lobsters in a fish tank.

Like many women in their mid-thirties, I'd already faced, more than once, this shift in dynamics with other expectant friends. My husband and I had decided not to have children right around the time more and more of our friends vanished from our social circle into parenthood. To say that these shifts were easy on me would be untrue. I knew it would take at least two years after Max's baby was born (worst case scenario: five) before the quake squared off and the earth beneath her feet settled. Face it, I told myself, her mother's group is *in*. You're *out*.

"Oh, Max, I'm so happy for you!" I cheered, way too energetically, guilt rising in me until I felt like the worst, most insincere friend ever. I was much too flustered to be genuine.

So what about Max's decision made me fear I would be evicted from her life and that our friendship would wither, cell-by-cell? And by this I mean, what word or emotion would I call it, exactly?

I'm not sure. Recognizing an emotion doesn't always translate into defining one. That much I do know. Feeling is more powerful than explanation — it's what we have when there are no words.

Max and I met in our early thirties. We were both childless *by choice!* Something I said frequently in those days with an exclamation point hitched to the end just to be sure people *got it!* All through that proving-myself decade, I found I was justifying, to others as well as to myself, my career goals and aspirations, void of any real maternal longings, in a way a man would never need to. The common theme in the lives and thoughts of most of my friends and family was *it is time to have a baby.*

It occurs to me that, at the time, I thought things for my generation had changed from that of my mother's. I was fooled. In many circles, the underlying message remained that it's not entirely socially correct behavior for a woman of childbearing age to be overly enthusiastic and determined to keep reaching for possibilities instead of Pampers. Or too openly ambitious and excited about her career goals, aspirations, and successes.

Either subtly or flat-out blatantly, I was told by many that I would eventually give into my biological time clock, put my career on hold, and level the parental playing field. And there was this tiny part of me that believed it, too.

"You'll change your mind," my mother kept saying.

"The day will come when you'll want a baby more than another book published," a friend said. This to a writer? Some friend.

"But you *are* going to have a baby someday, right?" another friend said. Her words surprised me the most. She'd been the wild child of our college set, but since marrying an extremely wealthy man from Iran she'd ... what? Retracted, or so it seemed to me. She didn't wear a chador or anything, but she no longer made many decisions on her own, either.

"In God's eyes, sex is for procreation, *capisci*?" That was my dad. Though his religiousness always seemed a little flimsy to me, seeing as how, for as far back as I can remember, he's spent Sunday mornings on the golf course. He's what my friend Jackie calls "a Christmas and Easter Catholic." And then there is the little matter of infidelity (see Chapter 3).

For whatever reason, having a baby never quite dove-tailed with my deepest desires. But that doesn't mean part of me, the ever-questioning part, the one that needs to weigh things out, didn't give the idea a lot of energy and time. Still, whenever I heard someone assume motherhood was a part of my future, I'd behave like my *most* woman-without-a-stroller self, trying as if with a cigarette to grind out their assumption. It didn't take much to trigger me, either. I'd defend my position until I sounded more like an advocate for choice rather than just one woman with her own set of hopes and wants.

Even from my most liberated set of friends, the message I received if I dared have the "mommy vs. non-mommy" con-versation was one of heedful warning. I wondered if their intent was to convince me that I'd miss out on something. And I would, of course. But wouldn't they, too?

The question I still ask myself: Why is it socially accept-able for mothers to say, like buzzards sensing weakness, things to childless women like, "You know, if you had chil-dren you couldn't accept that writing residency in Spain" as though that thought, that *freedom*, had never occurred to me? And yet, I fear the whole cosmic order of motherhood would swoop down on me in a mob if I dare spoke the words: "You know, you'd be able to apply to a writing residency in Spain if you didn't have that kid." Perhaps there is a good reason why mothers say these ridiculous things to non-moms. Maybe it's some kind of subconscious test because only the most committed friends would stand by each other after one too many of these are-you-going-to-be-more-like-me conversations.

The worst sting I ever had to endure was when a good friend said I'd out*grow* my work goals, implying immaturity was underlying my choice to be a writer (and at that time, also a dancer) instead of a mother. Who would ever say those words to a man? That pang still glares at me from the back of my mind. I suppose she needed to believe I'd eventually want to join the stroller brigade she and most of my other friends had formed in lieu of me.

To be fair (and kinder than I really feel), I think the point she needed to make, much like many of my ex-hippie friends, was something akin to birds need to fly, fish need to swim, and women need to give birth in order to carry out the most inherent truth of our DNA, stemming not only from history and tradition but a deeply held conviction (and scarily close to certain right-wing agendas) that all things essential exist in or are produced by nature *vis-à-vis* the womb.

In those days, in so many ways, I would leave a friend's home — usually following the dreaded question, "So, have you given any more thought to having a baby?" — perfectly drained, the spirit in me running out through the pores of my skin. When I felt like I had to stand up not only for what I wanted, but for who I was. As if the self-assured woman I thought I'd become was suddenly reduced to a fourteen-year-old wrangling for acceptance.

Not until I reached the age of forty did people come around. Suddenly (and what an abrupt difference there is between thirty-nine-and-three-quarters and forty) my friends and family accepted, without so much as a peep, my decision to opt for a baby-free future, most difficult for my mother, I imagine, eager for another grandchild to coddle.

Still, while some friends seemed a little worried for me or even, dare I say, a little put off by my choice — saying things like, "You know, you'd make the most wonderful mother!" which, by the way, I took as a compliment — not nearly as many, now thick into diapers and feeding schedules, poo-pooed my decision. In fact, many were giving my decision a nod. And from an honest few, expressing their own uncertainty about motherhood. Where I once heard only awe, I now heard admissions of things like boredom and tedium. I attribute a lot of this honesty to the writer Anne Lamont. Everyone was reading *Operating Instructions* back then, a journal of her son's first year. When I read it, I felt all of the mother-platitudes about what raising a child is supposed to feel like evaporate in the heat of her discoveries. I ate up everything else she wrote.

And, as long as I've steered us toward famous personalities, would someone please tell me why Oprah is so admired by mothers? What a contradiction to choose *not* to have a child while advocating, show after show, that motherhood is the ultimate experience for a woman. Isn't there something deliberately hypocritical about her saying that? Last time she repeated *motherhood is the ultimate experience for a woman*, I flicked off the set and I haven't given her an ear since, resenting such blatant audience-pandering. Let me ask you a question: Just how many mothers has she had on the cover of her magazine?

That was totally off the subject. I'm sorry.

Like I was saying, suddenly some of my new-mother friends and I could laugh again, or cry, or both simultaneously. Us, ever-emotional. Because the initial stage of born-again motherhood had collided with reality: unconditional love mixed with an overwhelming challenge. And within this clash, there's room for a non-mother like me, room that matches the pluses and many minuses of my own life, room to be reminded of what had brought us together in the first place.

How well Max and I thought we knew ourselves in those early days of our adulthood. And a large part of what we shared included not wanting to become mothers or as we saw it then, unimaginative. Maybe even powerless. Max was beginning a career as a photographer and we were in the throes of collaborating on a commemorative show portraying, through her portraits and my writing, ten well-respected women in our community. *So this is what it's like talking true with another artist*, I thought appreciatively every time we exchanged ideas about how that show would unfold.

I want to share with you a poem I wrote about those first meetings when we discussed not only the ten women we would honor but every other detail specific to our own lives:

COLLABORATION — *for Max*

Our collaboration begins
with you, the photographer, coming over to my place
to discuss how it is we'll portray ten women we admire
using your portraits, my words.

How to capture more than faces, I say,
how to pull a precise moment from her life,
widen it between us until there is access, something real
poking through as if yellow does a strip tease, revealing red
panties on a green bed of silk.

At least that's what I think
I meant, but sometimes with me
after that second glass of wine it's hard to tell ...
ideas start to rise and swarm until I'm torn
between lavishing attention on every idea I meet
or ignoring them altogether.

After that, the photographer who is also my friend
and I switch subjects to focus on the next level of success
we can't seem to generate on our own,

a little like standing on a shore and letting the waves
of insecurity lap at us as we continue
down the horrible road
where some better thing is always round
the bend of wanting but not getting.

For which want is *the* feat and,
for that matter, which compromise?

Perhaps more important is that, wine
or no, I could crawl into this kind of conversation,
(this tunnel of things we store away
just to stay on the safe side),
and live for days.

I still treasure the conversations I shared with Max, the only
working artist/non-mother I knew at the time. A woman who
dreaded baby showers and *All-Ages, No Alcohol* potlucks as
much as I did. We brought out the best in each other. Finally,
I remember thinking, I could share my thoughts about not
having a baby with someone without wondering if I'd
offended her in some misinterpreted way.

"You're both married women of childbearing age working at your art when most of your friends are exchanging
their purses for diaper bags. That can't be easy." That's what
an older woman said to me at our opening. I just stared at
her. She was so completely right it floored me.

Max, like me, was adamant about not wanting to give in
to motherhood or what, in our minds, still seemed like an easier, safer path than seeing our careers through. Seeing as how,

one by one, the pitfalls of trying to get ahead in our careers had begun to rise ever so clearly. Still I thought neither of us longed to take our work off our hands. While we shared an affection for our friends who were leaving the workaday world to become mothers, we made a pact to forge on without ever having to shop for a Snuggli.

Then it happened.

Max reached the ledge, jumped, and was now swimming in the deep waters of pregnancy where I couldn't tread. And there was this lump inside me making it painfully clear that I had to pull myself out of feeling left behind and into the height of empathy if our friendship was to survive. If I was ever going to look back on these days and say with an aren't-I-funny smile, "Remember when you got pregnant and I completely freaked out about it?"

Empathy: *The ability to understand another's needs, to listen and care about what another is going through.* Man, it's what I needed. Because dread was leaking in from all sides. And I was not proud of myself for it. It was as if, suddenly, I was carrying every other friendship disappointment around like a pebble in my Franco Sartos. I began to walk very carefully in and around my friendship with Max.

The saying goes: Every friend serves a different purpose. Some are there for us, some are there with us, and some need our help. As I see it, with Max and me, the shift between us was figuring out which we would be (and become) for each other. Until she became pregnant, I think we traversed all three in relation to our needs at the time. But now I sensed I could no longer be with or for her in the way she needed. She would need women going through the same life change as she. Because even the best, most trusted friend, if that friend has never been pregnant, is not enough support for a woman pregnant for the first time. I *wanted* to be enough for her. But the only words that slid out of me were *I'm not.*

Hence, Max's mothering group was born and I was now on the outside looking in at my friend's social life. Knowing there was no part of me that belonged to that Mother World, I needed to move along. Not in an angry way, I told myself angrily, but com*passion*ately. And not by ending the friendship. I knew we'd come back around. But to move into the next phase of our lives. Together, separately. Because there is *always* the next phase. I've been around long enough to realize this.

But moving on takes time. At first, I tried to keep things the same between us. I couldn't change what was overnight, so I wobbled our conversations back and forth for a while, trying to set us free carefully. Like moving a stove. And weird, but I never mentioned my fears. I like to think I express myself well, but every time I saw her I said nothing of how I was really feeling. A fat lot of good it did me.

For the first trimester I believed I was doing the right thing by my friend. I was full speed ahead in every obvious way. Which is a bit like having patience on uppers.

The problem is, it's difficult to maintain an honest friendship if your basic premise is keeping your real feelings under lock and key. "Still," I thought, "we will be the happiest pseudo-friendship *ever!*" I planned a baby shower with gusto. Me, the woman who dislikes baby showers more than going to the dentist. I tried to believe receiving blankets and toy-like clothes mattered to me. Their cuteness would keep us from drifting apart, right?

At the same time, I *was* writing about my fear of losing Max, expressing myself on the page rather than face to face. I admit, I'm too often guilty of this.

In real life, though, I pretended. She pretended. And we smiled a lot, like performers, grins on our faces soon as the lights pop up. But we both felt more and more detached from the friendship. If I said aloud my fears, I thought, entrusting them to the one person who might actually give a hoot, I'd have to act, wouldn't I? And I wasn't yet ready for that. I couldn't see my way into what I needed to do. I didn't want to let go. I didn't know that just admitting my fear was doing enough.

Anyway, we were *fine*, no boat rocking, as long as we stayed on the cuddly-baby subjects. Nothing too stretch-marky. Or real. Or, presto, I was acutely aware of how much I missed her (us) in the old sense of who we were. My mind would dip down around my solar plexus trying to protect my emotions. But there is no protection against loss.

Perhaps there is truth to the adage that the one outcome you most fear is the result you will create. Or is it that you can expect the best or fear the worst? Or is it that your deepest struggle will produce your greatest ..., oh, whatever the saying is, the point is the one thing I most dreaded about my connection with Max settled down to grow. On some self-destructing level, I suppose, it's reassuring to know the one thing you most fear exists after all. *See, I told you so!*

Then, just when I thought I had things, things like my *feelings* (good one), under control, a whole new set of events moved in and everything snowballed.

Of course it did.

The avalanche occurred one night as I hosted a party in my home, something I used to do with far more frequency before I turned, for whatever reason, out of my need to entertain so much. Along with several other friends, I invited a close friend who was, coincidentally, also pregnant for the first time. Max and she had not met before so they honed in on each other like two blonde Americans traveling through Greece.

An hour into the evening, after sitting around the fireplace with my other guests, I walked into my bedroom and there my two pregnant friends were, lying on my comforter, curled into each other like lovers, cooing and commiserating about all the changes their bodies were going through. I remember how the sound of their laugher, so elated, so shared, aroused a heap of jealousy inside me. I hadn't laughed like that with Max in a while. Had she been saving it up? Had we forgotten how along the way?

I'm a little ashamed to admit how their instant bonding hurt my feelings. I felt out of the loop, out of *my* loop, left behind. Which made me a little nervous. And when I'm nervous, I talk, actually, I run off at the mouth, my mind racing through a backlog of words searching for something, *any*thing to say. Unless I'm able to rein myself in so I might speak from a place other than speed. Unfortunately, this hardly ever happens.

My first reaction was to sit on the edge of the bed and instantly, as if sprung from a cannon, alter their intimate alignment. To wiggle my way in enough to be part of the thread.

Why? Resentment, fear, envy?

Yes! And twice more yes. And yes!

The nerve of them! The gall!

I started running off at the mouth, my voice about four octaves above normal. As I remember it, I said something about artistic process (huh?), something about my work and what part about it was bringing me the most conflict blah, blah, blah. I *knew* what I was doing was inappropriate, but knowing it only seemed to fan it. I kept looking at Max for reinforcement. *Remember this life we used to share?*

"Uh-huh," she responded after too long a pause. And that settled everything to my end of the conversation. They stared at me. *Go away*, I could hear them thinking, *so we can talk about placentas.* The room seemed to melt in that moment and I was a second away from tears. "Oh. Um. K. Well," I mumbled. I stood, walked into the bathroom, a deflated balloon.

I was past tense. The two of them shared the same hearth.

Another message made clear in that embarrassing moment: What brought meaning to my life was no longer part of the equation for either friend. Which may sound unimportant. Or even selfish compared to what pregnant women go through to bring the next generation into the world, but there you have it. Max and I had shot for opposite stars. We were no longer in the same orbit. We couldn't regain one another. She couldn't share her bodily changes with me any more than I could physically understand them. And though I'd hoped our friendship would trump the divide, inside I knew this was not to be.

Right then and there, I released my two friends to each other. Emotionally, though, I backtracked. Way back. Memories like *I won't get asked to the dance!* and *the popular clique is making fun of my kinky hair!* were making their way up my spine, dire and razor-sharp. I was a grown woman, yet there I was insecurely interpreting love just like in seventh grade, feeling there is only so much of it to go around.

I thought that if my friends chose each other, they would let go of me. I sat on my toilet and cried a good long cry. The hostess on hiatus from her own party. No one ever died from this passage, I told myself while sitting in my privy. Because if they did, I'd have keeled over several friend- ships ago.

And so, I accepted, with an eerie new-calmness, that our bond might hold up *over time* but at present, the best thing I could do for my friend was to step aside. Then, with another breath and my jeans down around my ankles, I cried some more. Emptied myself. Drained the reservoir that was, it felt like, every sorrow ever lodged in me.

About half an hour went by. Then, apart from my breath- ing, which was still not going all the way down to my lungs, I think my vital signs were returning quite normally. And it struck me that I wasn't going to cry one more tear. There was still a tiny nibble of pride left in me and I was going to draw from that. And I meant it. I *meant* it. With that, a release of a zillion insecurities that can harass the mind overwhelmed me, moving through every nook of my body. It was definitely physical.

All right then, I thought, maybe this is how people feel when they undergo an out-of-body ... whatever it's called. Or maybe I was just exhausted. Cried out. Pathetic. Either way, I decided, that resignation is easier on me than fear.

Under my breath like a prayer, I whispered *okay*.

It's all so beyond our control. In my moment of privy-illumination, I finally got that so much about life is knowing when to hold on and when to let go. I left the bathroom and returned to my other friends waiting in the living room, and over the next months I gave myself more freely to them. And by doing so, I was also freed from my clingy need to define friendship by the past, aka Max.

Now, years later, my friendship with Max is revived, maybe even stronger. And the best part is we don't try to recreate our past friendship. I doubt either of us remembers just how we were back then anyway. I think Ingrid Bergman put it perfectly when she said, "Happiness is good health and a bad memory."

And, at the time of this writing, I'm honored to be the most fun babysitter to her two young boys. Which means I get to tuck them in way past bedtime after popcorn and M & M's for dinner, teach them that women are the stronger sex, and how to swear, though it's not my intention.

And day by year, baby by baby, book by book, we grow with each other's changes. Which means, for us both, a myriad of details to any given day. Nowadays what we share most, I think, is recognizing that we both have a lot of work ahead of us if we're going to pull off our lives as well as we want to. I've never asked her, but I think Max finds it as comforting as I do to have someone to gripe with who knows just how much we each went through to get here.

Which, by the way, is pretty incredible.

And I never mention two things (well, until now): The fantastic, luxurious sense of freedom that descends when I leave her home and enter a childless world by myself. Or that this peaceful sensation has been my *numero uno* form of birth control through the years.

If any one woman's story seems to stand out from all the others, for me, it's this one: A jewelry designer in her mid-thirties living in Seattle had this to say about the pregnancy of her long-standing friend, and the transition she was trying to pilot her way through:

It was hard on us after the baby came. During her pregnancy, I didn't get the sense we were headed for trouble. Her bodily changes fascinated me. I liked talking about them.

Before the pregnancy, our friendship was less intense for a while when she got married. But that was easier. We had both reached a plateau of feeling like our careers weren't the most important thing in our lives anymore, so her shift of attention to this great guy was important. She was blissfully happy and her marriage gave me hope I'd find someone incredible, too.

But after the baby came, things started to — I don't know how to say this — run out? The first indication was when she gave me a framed picture of her baby for my birthday. I was like what the hell is this? I already had enough baby photos to fill an album of my own. I know this sounds trivial.

Then I began to notice — and maybe all mothers do this I don't know — that whenever we talked, all I'd get was this rundown on the kid. I mean his progress was interesting, not all that interesting really, but what I wanted was to be let in on how she was doing.

The one time I pointed this out, she got really mad at me. She said I didn't have a clue, yet. I loved that, "yet." And I thought, wait a minute, she is scolding me for saying what I felt. What gives? As if having a baby was a sacred experience, and my life was now ... what? Irrelevant?

I figured we'd get back on track eventually. But there was this inequity in how we showed each other support. I thought so, anyway. I still wanted to believe things would even up. Have you heard the expression "atheist with a lot of faith?" That's me.

"What do you mean by inequity," I asked. Knowing full well where she was headed.

I'll tell you. But you have to promise not to ....

"Judge you?" I finished her sentence. I need to get over this habit. It's rude. "I'm sorry I cut you off," I said. "I'm working on that."

What I was going to say was that you have to promise not to forget I'd let a bunch of these instances slide by already. Her son could say my name out loud and she still carried on like he was the throbbing pulse of the universe. I remember thinking this is why boys grow up with such confidence. They live like gods in the center of their mothers' worlds.

But I lost hope for us after my show. The first reputable show of my work in four years. Even though I'd been to two (which is one too many) T-ball games, birthday parties (three out of four, anyway) and a pre-school play. And yet, she couldn't make it to my show? She left a message, when she knew I'd be at my show, saying something had come up at home. I thought, that's it.

The night of my opening was such a high for me. Most of my pieces sold and there was a huge turn out. But I felt pretty depressed afterwards. And not just because of the letdown after all that build up. That's what still makes me so mad. That her not coming got to me that way. It took away some of the good stuff I should have been feeling.

I wish I could say I have a happier ending for you, but I'm good with my decision. Especially when I heard she was pregnant again. I can't fake my enthusiasm for it.

Understanding her feelings was easy for me. So much of friendship is about showing up. Still, I think most women find it too hard to bring up any unfairness we feel. Resentment builds. I asked her why she hadn't let on about her feelings.

You have to both want to figure out what's going on. And I did-n't get any indication she did. So I made a conscious effort to stop focusing on us, to let it all sort of breathe for a while. Honestly, it was a huge relief to be done with all that, that ....

"... disappointment?" Oh. Damn! I did it again.

Yes!

We fell silent, the kind of silence filled with all that's been said.

What a fascinating opportunity presents itself here, I thought, my old journalist-mind kicking in. To get the other side of how this friendship broke down was the next step lined up and waiting. I asked if she minded if I gave her friend a call to hear her side of the story.

No. But spare me what you find out. I'm on a roll. I'm dating someone really great. And I found a rep for my designs. I want to stay focused on these two parts of my life right now. I want to savor it.

Who couldn't relate to that?

I was nervous about calling her friend. I could think of so many reasons why this woman wouldn't want to talk to me. Then I rallied my courage, phoned her, and left a mes-sage. I waited. A week went by. I didn't want to call again, cer-tain she didn't want to talk to me. And why would she? I was a stranger who wanted details about her private life. And not for discreet reasons, but to *publish* them. And I came loaded with an ear-full from her ex-friend. Oh, brother, I thought, like she'll call. I'd worked it all out in my mind. She'd never call back.

But in the middle of the second week, she did call back, explaining with a laugh that she wanted to phone when she was alone and not chasing her son around. Which was not often, she added.

I also suspected she needed time to absorb my message and to think clearly about what she wanted to say.

After I filled her in, reading aloud from my notes, there was a long, rather awkward hush on the line. *Having to pretend that we still had anything in common was exhausting,* she finally said.

Then with no added prompting, she took in a breath and went on: *I don't want to sound like I'm defending myself but I think* (another long pause) *that she is right about the inequality, and I'm not just saying that because I know she'll read this. She showed me far more support than I was able to give back. I just ran out of steam for so many things after my son was born. I think I was depressed, though at the time I thought I was just tired. And now, between my son who never stops and my baby on the way, I don't have anything left. Oh, and there's my husband. Which is exactly how he feels most of the time now: overlooked. And if I do have a flicker of time to myself, I want if for myself, not to try to catch up with someone else. Especially someone who is always doing something a little hipper than anything I can relate to anymore and has so much going on and needs so much affirmation about all of it. I think she needs me as an audience more than a friend. That sounds mean.*

I thought we were done and I was beginning to sense she was no longer in the mood for this phone conversation. Something in her tone made me think either I or the effort was beginning to grate on her nerves.

It's more than that, she continued. Oh good. I held my breath. Something was about to break ground.

There just comes a point. You can spend too much time trying to get it right. I was trying and failing, trying and failing. I've thought

about how if I'd been more attentive, more into her jewelry, more sis-
ter-like, funnier, less into my son, less intense, should I go on?

We laughed.

I can't go back into that world of meeting for a drink and discussing
a million topics in an hour, shopping for clothes, visiting a gallery, all of
it, all the things we used to do together, because now, and this is hard to
say, I miss all that sometimes. But I don't miss it if I stay in my world.

Here is where I really identified with her. In the compet-
itive ring others like to call a writing community, there is that
one thing you hear about that someone else is doing or getting that can completely turn your good day into an insecure
one. If I stay focused on my work, I don't feel jealous or envi-
ous. But if I read about another writer's accomplishments —
a writer, say, way up there on the totem — oh, man, sometimes I can feel so *un*accomplished.

It wasn't her fault that I'd sink into this melancholy when I was
with her. I don't want to feel like I'm missing out on something. It's
not fair to my family. So I removed myself. I don't know why I let
some people affect me this way. She isn't the only one.

So why not have this conversation with her? I asked.

I didn't want to, so I hedged. Eventually she got the message.
And I got what I wanted even though I didn't have the guts to say it.
I don't want you to think I am not happy with my life.

I asked if she thought the friendship would ever find its
way back.

Probably not. Maybe if she has a few kids and moves out here
to Redmond.

Again we laughed. But I couldn't say what I was thinking:
That this was a story I savored.

After we hung up I thought about the two of them, that
if only they'd sit down and share with each other what they
shared with me, their friendship might make it.

But maybe not. Perhaps both are doing exactly right by
themselves.

I suddenly can't believe how little I know, for sure, about anything of what it takes to cement a friendship for good.

And for some odd reason, that feels like a relief.

Oh, wow, did the T-ball story above trigger my own embarrassing T-ball memory. I'd stuffed it way back. If I could, I'd delete it for good.

When I went to my one and only T-ball game (I didn't even know what T-ball *was*), it was a terrifying experience. I, too, went to be a supportive friend because I love Max and her sons without reserve. What I remember most vividly is the terror that struck me soon as I looked around from out-of-bounds. I was the only woman-without-child in a swarm of young parents (and, ah, *not*-so-young parents). It seemed like the whole normal world had completely passed me by. I was the odd duck. Again. Just like in high school. And I had two simultaneous feelings playing bumper car in my head: the first was that I'd made a terrible mistake by not having a baby, and, secondly, that the whole mommy-daddy-T-ball world might be contagious if I stayed a second longer!

I wound up fleeing on my bicycle before my friend's son even got his turn at bat. Later I tried to apologize in a tearful phone message, "I loved the game, but ...," I lied. I don't remember what other lie I made up about my fast-flying exit. I didn't *want* to lie to my friend, but I wasn't sure telling the truth would improve the situation that's for sure. It's amazing, isn't it, how much duplicity it takes to keep things humming along?

The whole tiny time I was at the game I kept hearing *woman-without-offspring meets reproductive world* in my head. I started to doubt my choices. My ability to enjoy the game for what is was, which was my friend's world, pulled quietly shut.

The grown-up me knew better, but I don't need to tell you how present Ms. Doubtfulness was just then. She was big at my side, gigantic, and spreading her apron wide. I had to climb out of those folds and tell myself, over and over, that I loved my life, my quiet writer's life. And not one of us can have it all *all* of the time.

I never told Max all the things that raced through my head that day.

I think here about our need to protect ourselves from people and situations that, for whatever reasons, cause us to turn our life decisions into opponents. The women above helped me see how there isn't one way in which we see ourselves, there's a lot of questioning going on, no guarantees that we will never doubt our choices. It's more about sizing up the pluses against the minuses, I think. Maybe we, any of us, aren't entitled to more.

As I sit watching birds fly in and out of the feeder that hangs in front of my office window to remind me just how fragile everything is, this is what comes: Losing my way with Max and then reconnecting taught me how to be more patient with my friends as they weave through their own transitions.

So thank you Max. Even though you had no idea at the time how much you were stirring up that moon-lit night you smooched it up without your panties on.

And your life forever changed.

ULTRASOUND — *for Max*

Now that you are gloriously rounded,
the weight of your child exposed,
recurring questions surface and break
like waves into fear: *Between us, will a chasm fan out?*
You on one side with child,
me on the other?

As your belly
(stretched for one more life to lie beneath)
is spread with gel,
it startles you and bothers me
no one in the hospital's orbit
thought to warm the tube.

A bitter, hygienic smell wafts up.
Suddenly, my thighs ache for no good reason.
I knead them
relieved when a sensor rolls over your abdomen.
I feared a needle the size of a pen
was about to pierce flesh.

But that's the *other* test. Amnio-something.
I'm new at this.

Too, I'm a knot of concern at your side, my eyes
fixed on a silent screen
where fluids rise black
so bladders and bellies are dark
bobbing dots no larger than dimes.

Ah. A blur becomes a body:
heart pulsing, layers of rib, arms extended
as if to hold our gaze.

Oh!

Two legs, yikes, with a third between.
We grin like voyeurs, drink in the news.
It fills us.

When the monitor dissolves
into static we say how we want our boy back
on our side of life. All of him
wrapped in flannel.

I can see, as you smooth the printout
like Braille beneath your fingers,
he is the reason you live now
as much as the air. So I step in closer
to hug you. At the same time, I move away
just a little and
just for now

SIX

On Transition

*"Men kick friendship around like a football
and it doesn't seem to crack. Women treat
it like glass and it can fall to pieces."*

— ANNE MORROW LINDBERGH

The sun is just now rising. A perfect star heats up the morning. From my balcony, the city lies beyond: Elliott Bay to my left with a ferry just now pulling in, and to my right, a view of Queen Anne Hill in various shades of gray and green. How I love it here. Even before moving to Seattle, I remember walking its sidewalks, looking up at a Juliet balcony much like the one I now stand on and I knew this would be me one day.

But there's another reason I like to stand out here before I begin my workday: When I pause to lay my eyes on the morning, the rest of my day falls into place. Standing here requires I take the time to reflect and take pride in my accomplishments instead of wanting for more. Because as soon as I sit at my desk, want returns. By way of a sentence, another page, the next book eager to be written. I can mark my life by my titles. It's all there, the beginnings and ends of me meeting between the book covers.

Still, as beautiful as the city is from up here, it's not yet *my* city. I'm still trying to claim it as my own sense of place, still trying to make Seattle my home. So if my eyes aren't drawn to Elliott Bay, then I look up at the ever-changing sky, or below at the rush of traffic on Fifth Avenue (which always makes me appreciate that I can work from home) to help me feel grounded. Not an easy thing when one lives this high up. Five flights is a long way for roots to travel.

And though this morning is nearly perfect in all the visual ways that feed me, I don't relish how I went to bed last night, with a vague sense of panic that I'd said everything I want to say on the subject of friendship, and that there's nowhere for me to go in this closing chapter. It seemed to me that I'd questioned (and answered) enough. Silver linings are my pet peeve, so no part of me wants to write a corny wrap-up and call it a day. As tempting as this sounds.

In fact, when I first started this book, one of my dearest friends told me she wouldn't read a book like this one, mine or anyone's. To her, the whole notion of understanding ourselves through our friendships is boring "unless you're willing to go where I'm afraid to." I admit her words have hummed in the background of my thoughts through these pages, urging me to get down in there deeper.

So why the unease last night? Shouldn't it just be easy to end with this new confidence I feel because I've stayed with these chapters long enough to let them lead me to the friends I found and explain why I lost others. Long enough to know how disappointing it feels to promise myself I'll do things differently from now on and then chicken out, not bother to, or still not know *how* to. Long enough to be aware of certain behaviors I'd like to outgrow, and then, while licking my wounds, I watched a few of them reverse into old bad habits. But not all of them. And that's something. Really, it's a lot.

"There is something else I need to say about all of this, but I don't know what it is," I tell Larry over coffee.

"It'll come to you," he says.

"I feel it picking up but there's no wind."

The color in his cheeks deepen. He's afraid, yes he is, that I'll turn this little stir into a gale just to avoid going to work. With good reason. Like most writers, I have a love/hate relationship with my desk. There are mornings I'll do anything to avoid it. Even pick a fight with the man I love.

"Okay, bye, good luck!" he says. I know him so well. He's revving up his false cheerfulness to even out the doubt he can see in my eyes. At times like these (there are many), I can't conceal my fear that I'm not a Real Writer. It hides in plain view. It makes us both jumpy.

"Thanks," I say. I kiss him on the cheek. He can't get away fast enough. But instead of sitting down to reenter my work, I go to my friend Jeane's blog, then a little on-line shopping (cashmere for thirty bucks!). I download Martha & The Vandellas: *Callin' out around the world, are you ready for a brand new beat?* (I used to dance all over my room to this song. I know better than to question why, even now, it makes me feel more alive. I absolutely have to own it again.) Jeane would say I'm letting life get in the way. But I know I'm wasting time.

When I think about the last few weeks, how I keep referring to my pages of notes, but, yet, I can't sink into what I need to say next, can't string together a single sentence, I feel locked up. My fingers are ready to fly across the keyboard, but I'm stuck.

I remind myself that stillness is exactly what needs to happen. That sometimes the most basic things are beyond words. Beyond words? Oh, great. What kind of comfort is that to a writer?

And then, this bright morning, the phone rings. Oh, good, I think, with relief. If it's Jeane, this will take up most of the morning!

It *is* Jeane. I didn't know when I answered that she'd be the wind I've been waiting for, my break in the clouds. But I'm not surprised. Our conversation kicks me into forward motion. She is just that kind of friend.

Then something else, clear as the city from my terrace, shifts into view. I could go on and on about where it came from, but the important thing is that I was finally able to meet myself in this final chapter.

Some phone conversations leave me wondering about all the subtle facial expressions I missed, the grins and nods that help me know what someone is really trying to say. I think about the words, how they need to travel over thousands of miles of tangled wiring, how susceptible to misunderstanding this divide can make them, misconceptions that can wake me at 3:00 a.m. to wonder *what did she mean by that?*

Not so with Jeane. How good I feel in her company. Even on the phone. It's an easy jump to get to us. It's the purest freedom. Whenever something uncomfortable comes up between us, Jeane dives right in. Or I do. Honestly, I've never had a friendship willing to chance the uncomfortableness before. Not that these exchanges make us special: I don't know anyone who doesn't *want* to communicate well, but it takes a lot of courage (and time) to have these kinds of conversations. So although we've survived a few complicated hurdles like personal changes, my relocating, both of us caring for aging parents, our own aging so that what really concerns us shifts all the time, we're still standing.

And it's not as if we are all that much alike. We've piled up our pasts into very different bundles. Her bundle includes two grown sons and grandchildren she adores. Yet, through all our segues, we've made time. I'm proud of us.

The biggest thing I learned from our friendship (so far) is how to be true even about our dark sides. We don't dip into something arousing, and then circle back to safe ground quick as we can. This was new terrain for me. At first, I didn't know that the reason I was so attracted to this level of openness was that I wanted to write a book from the viewpoint of a woman who believes two things: The only point of writing is to be honest. And the only point of friendship is the same.

I don't want to backtrack here, but what Jeane and I share, even long-distance, is my template for the future. I know who I am. I know the woman I want to become. Our talks don't let me forget.

Back to the light-shedding conversation. The first words out of Jeane's mouth were these: "You almost done with that book about friendship?" Yet, at the same time, I detect a little hesitancy in her voice. My friends are sometimes wary of showing up in my writing. And why wouldn't they be? Friends and family are the story writers have.

"Funny you should ask," I say. "I'm working on the closing chapter. Or trying to."

"Well, I can't wait to read all about us then!" she adds. Her curiosity, which is really the highest form of generosity, is a gift. It's a relief to hear how quickly it replaces her reluctance.

Because do you know how many friends I've had who can embrace my work life with enthusiasm and make me feel I can do anything? Who would pay me a compliment like that? Wait, let me think back. Further back. Let's see. There. I count on one hand the people I've known who can dispense of a compliment easily, who can leave their insecurities out of the equation and genuinely give of themselves. This kind of support, like the dark color of her hair and lipstick, emphasizes who Jeane really is, and reminds me how a good friend is there for you when you seem to be succeeding, not just when you are needy.

And I *was* in need. Truth is I was scared, and I needed someone to remind me of all the other times I'd come just short of finishing a book and felt this same lack of confidence creeping in. Huge doubts that can leave me starved for a little encouragement.

"I've never had better friends since I stopped caring so much about having them. Jesus, has anyone?" Jeane says next.

My immediate reaction is to laugh.

This, I decide, is what I've been trying to describe, how we can make each other laugh and think about something so heavy at the same time. I brighten and feel all best-friendy inside. I know, I *know*. The grown up me doesn't *want* the whole best friend thing, that it took me years (and writing Chapter 4) to discover that a balanced life is more a matter of best moments with all kinds of friends. Thing is, so many best conversational moments have been with Jeane.

"I think," she adds, "you chose the subject because it's been ... what? Less than a year since you left this small town behind?"

This is, I realized in an instant, what I needed to confront: relocating, its effects on my friendships. How hard the transition was even though every ounce of me wanted it.

"It's going to be hard to go over the move while I'm still digging in," I said. "Usually I rely on a little distance before looking back."

"Here's what you do." she said. "Remember how you feel back stage just before you go on, how scared you are. But you have to make your entrance anyway. Tap into that." Jeane is a theater director. She often approaches our have-to's like a director would. Our lives/our stage. Her words were a beacon.

"Or when you first went away to college — remember how scared you were? But nothing would keep you from going."

Jolted again. I knew exactly where this chapter needed to go. Rarely in life does someone say the very thing that can grab you out of your sinking state and kaplunk you right down onto higher ground. Without Jeane, I'd be lost.

"You just popped me free," I said, trying to hide the fact that now I wanted to hang up and get back to work right away.

"See you, bye." Without words, she knew.

I was terrified of going to college. Still I would count the days. Because another part of me couldn't wait to get out there. I was hungry for all kinds of new things back then, as now, leaving a small town in Connecticut to attend college in the heart of Boston. I also remember that in the shadowy hours just before dusk, my fears of not fitting in or being able to compete would echo from the depths of me. Still I couldn't let fear stop me. Where would we be, any of us, if we let fear stop us?

My mom and I said our good-byes on the slate steps that led up to my townhouse dorm on Commonwealth Avenue, hugging awkwardly, looking at the center strip of green that was now to be my only contact with the concept of a yard. As soon as she was out of sight, I went into my room, sat on my bed, looked around at my new world, and broke down crying. I was sure I'd flunk out, that my roommates would hate me, or I'd get mugged in an alley. So many doubts had mixed with so much elation and the jumble sent me into a tailspin.

Even now, too much of both is a recipe for disaster in terms of my ability to focus. But with time, I've come to recognize what I couldn't then: that eventually this sudden rush of insecurity evaporates into a seed of follow-through. Even if it doesn't feel like it initially, it's just the incentive I need. Once I override it, it becomes my flagstone. Then I take the next wobbly steps forward, double-daring myself all the way.

Now comes the admission: Yes I am the woman on the balcony in the opening paragraph, happy to have relocated recently. Glad to be home on the fifth floor of a new building in a large and vital city rather than tending, as I had for so many years, a garden out my back door, until the day I recognized that my garden was flourishing beyond my grandest expectation ... but I was not.

My husband and I moved because I awoke one morning and could no longer endure living in a small town west of Seattle. For years I lived a comfortable life there in a lovely cottage. Perhaps too comfortable. After nearly two decades, all the familiarity grew to be annoying, just the way none can. On top of that, there was something even more nagging: a persistent ache in me to reach beyond a small town's borders.

Working as a writer had shown me how to work hard, work scared, work confused and embarrassed and feeling like a foolish failure. I figured it was time to do the same with my future. Just your run-of-the-mill identity crisis but after searching for a community where, ultimately, no matter where you live, there is only the one you create, I figured it was time to make mine where I didn't feel like I was living with half a heart in terms of enthusiasm.

Still, there is always the emotional wrestle of starting over. It's challenging and exhausting to seek and build friendships in a city where you don't know anyone other than your husband and your realtor. Working through this passage with its many disappointments and discoveries tested my self-confidence daily.

Now, a year later, I feel I've finally made the transition. Daily routines feel normal. But it's been more difficult in some ways than I've let on to others and myself. Mostly because I'm better at facing these sorts of challenges alone. I'm not as afraid of them if I don't talk them to death. I need more of a quiet connection to what I want for myself. It steers the way.

My first months in the city, I felt as though I'd liberated some long-repressed characteristic, a release of anonymity which I craved after living in a small town where, if you aren't bound and determined to live otherwise, over time, convention can reign in even the freest spirit. Small town reserve is a powerful equalizer.

And even if you aren't willing, on any terms, to *be* harnessed, you, especially as you grow older, and perhaps especially if you are a woman, eventually are referred to as a village "character." Not that there's anything wrong with village characters. The ones I've met are some of the most intriguing people I know. It's just that "character" is not a title I ever wanted for myself. I wanted to live, at least for the next phase of my life, where even the most absurd situation or person hardly warrants a second look, where real differences of appearance, background, and race are commonplace.

But there were days when this very release, this freedom I longed for, began to feel more like I was a figment floating over the sidewalks: *No one sees me because no one recognizes me.* And as I went about the hard work of sinking layers of new roots, which was difficult from a nest so high up, I had moments of almost debilitating longing for my old ones. Leaving behind older friendships and bridging new ones can drain even someone as determined as I am. It's the constant effort of introducing yourself, retelling your "how I ended up here" story, and trying to get to know people that makes it hard to relax in the way you can with old friends. There's more of a sense of presenting yourself, which is its own pressure.

Still, there is a rich quality to anonymity. But how I missed some of my old familiar friends.

True, too, that too *many* attachments and social commitments can knock me off balance. Life in my small town had become too much build up of routines I no longer enjoyed, not enough down time, so that I would fret about too many unimportant things. I found it harder and harder to see into a clear vision of where I wanted to go in my life. Difficult to envision the woman I wanted to be because I was so distracted by the woman I *was*. There were too many layers of familiarity clouding my focus. Still, those layers were in place. They formed a circle of safety. I knew them for what they were, inside and out. And I knew myself well within them.

Which is why, after my initial rush of excitement when I viewed every Seattle discovery with the wide-eyed glee of a tourist, being unplugged from my friends and routines began to disconnect me from my most confident self. This feeling, it turns out, was the most difficult stage of relocating. Finding my way out of these emotions was a new-to-me and demanding challenge.

Then the most surprising thing happened: this disconnect made me begin to question my own like-ability, which, in turn, caused me to feel a little unworthy of making new friends. It doesn't matter that the feeling was ungrounded, the message still chipped away at my self-esteem. The plain fact is that this feeling would eat through me sometimes. Fear replaced excitement. I felt lost and rootless. Once, I sat on the floor of my kitchen repeating these words: *the only way to the other side of emotions is to get through them, and there are no shortcuts* — who said that?

But I'm hardly alone. So many in Seattle are searching for friends, trying to get to know someone over coffee at Starbucks. I figured if they could get to know one another, so, eventually, could I. Because, gratefully, it's not the kind of city where your family needs to go back a generation or no one will talk to you. People *want* to talk to you. At least the people in my neighborhood do. There are more and more new immigrants on my streets every day, lonely beyond what I'll ever experience. They are eager to assimilate, looking for someone willing to guide them, talk to them, accept them, help them test their communicativeness in a language difficult to master. Several have become friends and I think finding them was a huge gap I needed to fill, as I, too, am only first generation in this country, never fully rooted or at home as I'd like to feel.

There's Bali from Pakistan. He's one of the kindest, funniest people I've ever met. He runs a private post office on Second Avenue and I find myself holding on to my outgoing mail, not willing to drop it in my lobby's mailbox, just so I can mail it from his business where part of his determination is to make his customers laugh, a quality I find irresistible in another. And rare. Especially in Seattle, which is usually more inhibited, every crook of it.

And Roya, from Iraq, makes the most amazing food at her restaurant around the corner from my building. I wish, at this writing, I could remember the name of my favorite, a flaky spinach and cheese-filled dumpling that, upon tasting, made me clap with delight. Yet, as incredible as her food is, it's not her cooking that draws me to her café. It's the stories of her homeland, her openness about what it's like to find herself living in this country as an Iraqi woman, especially at this time in history. How grateful she is to be here in this new, accepting city, alive and unafraid. And I adore it when her grandchildren visit the restaurant. You can hear their high-spirited laughter, their playfulness in the air, a relief of sound in this mostly childless core of our city where the only other high-pitched sound one hears is another truck backing up.

And Amagit, pronounced *A-mah-geet,* from India. I've watched her transform in the year I've known her from tentative salesgirl to a confident fashion-plate working in a major department store downtown. She talks so appreciatively about the freedoms we women have in this country that she keeps me from taking them for granted. I remember when she said, "I can divorce my husband if the day comes I can't stand him any longer, and everyone in my caste won't reject me. Can you imagine? Do you know how freeing this is?" Then, quite quickly, she added, "Not that I want to do this," because she is still fearful I'll judge her honesty as a flaw in the perfect picture she says Indian women are taught from birth to present to the world. "Back home, we must live like old sick trees," she said. "Standing tall and proud on the outside. Even if our life is decayed from within. You mustn't ever take your freedoms for granted." And every time she says something like this, I want to capture and write it, just to remind women who swear they are not feminists that we could so easily slide back in time if we aren't fully aware and adamant, just like so many women in other countries have. Most of all, I love how Amagit, without flinching, looks me dead in the eyes when she tells me her secrets. She and I fascinate each other. We make each other *think*.

All of us are new to the city, either by choice, which is so much easier than being an immigrant it goes without saying, or in order to survive; so we try, best we can, to engender the care an inner city neighborhood needs if we don't want to feel alone in this world.

"God," I sighed into the receiver to my mom, "I didn't think it would be so hard to meet people."

"It's not hard to meet them," she said, newly relocated herself. "But most of them you don't want as friends, trust me."

That made me laugh. And I thought: *Wait until she reads Chapter 3.*

"It's harder for you," she continued, "because most people your age aren't relocating yet. They're still paying for their kid's college tuition, trying to pay off the mortgage. You and Larry are different that way. You didn't have kids, so this transitional time in your life came sooner. Most people wait until they retire. You're ahead of the curve my dear. You didn't wait because you didn't have to wait. But friendship, the closeness you're lonely for, takes years."

My jaw dropped open. I felt my hopes deflating. I didn't want to stay in this limbo between homes and friendships, this uncertainty, for *years*.

For the first time, I made myself come to grips with the fact that by pulling up stakes and moving to the city, perhaps I'd done the wrong thing. No matter how many life-changing risks others had taken and survived, maybe, this time, I just wasn't up to it.

"Hang in there. You always get what you need for yourself; you always have, ever since you were a kid. You aren't one of those people who whine just to whine and then don't make any changes because all they really want is pity."

Yep, I thought, diligent, persevering me. Sinking my claws in and not letting go.

"I know you can do it, you'll be fine," she said.

"I know, too," I said, not convinced.

My answer was more of a whitewashed-for-Mom kind of reply, because *fine* never feels quite right to me. Or truthful. Still, these days, I have some pretty grounding conversations on the phone with my mother. For some reason, we do better on the phone than when we meet up. Maybe it's because, on the phone, we both come to the conversation from our own home, our own, and best, sense of self and place.

"And, unlike me, you *have* time. Honey, I'd trade places with you in a heartbeat."

I too soon hung up the phone. I've not yet been able to join in the conversation that implies the all-too-real demise of my eighty-year-old mom. The thought of her not being around to talk to is too much for me. It's the future I don't want to see into. Loving her, *appreciating* her in the way she deserves, is unfinished business, no matter how many years I've spent trying. And failing. When she talks of her impending death, it's too close-up. It makes too dim the view of The Rest of My Life as I still need to see it, the many things I still need from her. And need to give back. The haziness stays with me for days and blurs everything.

Next time she brings up the inevitability, however, I want to be a better friend. Talk to her the way I talk to Jeane. Or try, at least. See where it goes. Encourage her to talk more about dying when she brings it up. Ask questions. Because of the transitions she faces every day, her life's fading into the past is so many millions times tougher than the transition I am facing. Mine, a new social circle. Hers?

I love her so much, and have, at times, known myself so little that I've spent a lot of energy needing to make her my opponent, my opposite, or else ... what? Become her? A daughter's need to see herself as separate from her mother in order to find herself has got to be the most painful part of the mothering cycle.

She was right about my move, of course. And in retrospect, I can see that the obstacles to moving at this stage of life, years before retirement, were there from the start. I just couldn't admit them. I was so eager to move on, to get back into some sort of anonymity, to ramp up my work, to experience life anew, nothing was going to stop me. Blind faith, I think, is our only choice and a powerful coping tool when we know we have to make a change.

Until something did stop me. And I was unnerved to discover just how lonely and homesick I was. Just like that, the tide turned from "Oh, I just love everything about my new life" to "Oh my God, did I make a mistake?" Now here I was, living in a tiny condo with no yard whatsoever, a move I would have never believed myself capable of a few short years ago. I missed the smell of grass renewing itself. And desperate for a firm, familiar place to stand on, I comforted myself with a writer's happy ending: *After I get through the worst of it, I'll write about it.*

"Homesickness" is the very word I resisted at first. I was unwilling to apply it to me. But we can't choose our feelings can we? We can hide them (though I'm not too good at that) but not select them from the others. Homesickness for a life I didn't want to return to is a difficult feeling to put a name to. It felt more like a blur in the center of me, not intentional but not unconscious either. I felt twinges of nostalgia between my hips, where want always moves in me. My work (this chapter) flowed around it, unable to anchor itself. It's not that any of my feelings of loss overwhelmed me by themselves. But they'd begun to add up.

I was in-between. Not homes exactly, but home-imaginings. Some call it nostalgia. Others, wistfulness. All I know is that, without a clue as to what the sentiment was, I sat at my desk in a fit of frustration trying to describe to the unafflicted how it felt to have a sort of homing impairment. Which had absolutely nothing to do with the subject of friendship. And *every*thing to do with it at the same time.

As I said earlier, the Portuguese have the perfect word for it: *Saudades: A sense of memory for something that might not even exist; still, you long for it all the same.* Oh, great, I thought, knowing how I can agonize over things only inferred or perceived, but still hurt so bad.

How I envy, at times, those rooted in this westernmost state. In their company I feel I live here, yes, but I am not *of* here. Part of the reason, I think, this homesickness swept over me, aside from my relocation, and irrespective of my restlessness-by-nature: I am a product of a free and privileged society blessed with a dizzying array of choices. The downside of this blessing? That there is always some new elusive possibility, ever enticing, right around the bend. Add that to how my imagination tends to stretch beyond measure, outpacing the reality of where I am with the possibilities of where I could *be*, and you have one big otherness, always.

So it looks as though I might be faced with home-befuddlement for some time to come because it occurs to me this might be nothing other than another one of life's many transitions forever taking me by surprise. That I simply need to brace myself in the waves, and hold steady.

And given a choice between an eternity or another passage-to-find-my-way-through, I'll gratefully go with the latter because the chances of my packing up and moving on are growing less and less now that I've finally found a sense of camaraderie in this city I chose. Which is no small solace to a writer who wants, once her workday is done, to step out of herself and onto sidewalks that feel comfortable and familiar.

And even if this confused sense of belonging arises from time to time, well, it's just the way life breaks through sometimes, isn't it? Just so we can peek inside.

None of this is exactly new and unique as far as experiences go. People are always striking out for new territory. Most of the time, when I stand in the elevator or at the post office swapping where-you-from stories, I find the people I thought of as "locals" have just relocated here before I did. So we are all visitors, really.

And the first time I had a party, my new home was full of apprentice-friends (as my friend, Diane, called them) as well as a few of my most coveted and seasoned ones (like her) willing to move, emotionally, that is, alongside of me. We danced the night away. My exuberance knew no bounds. I was so happy.

I have a photograph of that evening, all our arms waving in the air to the music. But I don't need the photo to remind me how happy I was to be dancing beside my "new" life. I remember.

When I do stare at the photo, though, I can make out how high my hopes for that evening were. My expectations were way up there. Did I expect too much from a party? I didn't think so. And it didn't let me down. That night was a crystallizing moment for me. Suddenly I did not doubt my choice to move away from a small town to find my home in the core of a city. Life is never certain. But on that evening, dancing on my beloved terrace, it seemed to be. "I'm on my way!" I told my husband.

And indeed I was.

I soon made another discovery: My husband and I have more of a social life in the city than we ever did in our small town where most everyone couples off to raise children, and the sidewalks are pulled in with the dinner hour. The first time I drove off the ferry at 10:30 p.m. and the sidewalks of downtown Seattle were still full of people, I felt a wonderful sense of excitement, the very thing that had been missing from my too-familiar life.

"You're still living on New York time," my hairdresser said to me. But it's not true. What he really means is something I readily admit, that I like exhilaration, the spring it puts in my step. I know no one can feel it always. Or continually. But neither am I willing to live without it. You can see it in people's eyes and posture, feel it in their attitude when they resign themselves, for whatever reason, to no real changes or future expectations. To me, making excitement a part of what I expect from life is an energizing challenge. It exhilarates me. It does not wear me out.

It feels wonderful to have survived the first year, to have weathered the unease long enough to allow something deeper to set in, the sense that I've done something to improve my life. Because what makes me the unhappiest, is any attempt to keep everything as it is, to keep the present tense a copy of the past with all my routines and friendships intact. There is no stopping time. Life keeps happening. The only grasp I can make on any of it is the next page I write.

These days, whenever I visit my old life in Port Townsend, I'm happy to be in my tiny cottage on ground level that roots me all over again, eager to revisit some of my old haunts and easy friendships, but I'm no longer at home there, not like I once was. In a sense, I grew up there, spent my twenties and thirties writing all morning in my pajamas, gardening in the afternoon, and directing a dance company in the evenings. It's not a chapter in my life that I'd redo if I could.

I enjoy returning because I've finally let go of an expectation that can drive me nuts, that there are any guaranteed ways to make a transition from old life to new. You just inch along until you do. And the thing is, every time I revisit my cottage-in-the-village, I find myself missing my nest in the city. A good sign. Because I'm convinced of something else now: that change is hard work, but it's not as hard as staying somewhere longer than you should. That's an important thing for me to keep in mind these days.

This morning, I find myself thinking about a few other things that happened over the past year in terms of making new friends, things I first learned as a girl, had to relearn in college, learn anew later in life (as I wrote in the opening chapter), and, so it seems, need to relearn again: that new relationships require finesse.

First of all, too much eagerness can scare a good prospect away. Once, on one of my speculative days, that is, one of my insecure days, I made the mistake of telling a woman who stood next to me in my neighborhood deli how lonely the city can feel at times. As if side-by-side made us confidants. I'm still so capable of misunderstanding proximity sometimes. But after she came back with a comment so fierce and irrational, something about how "newcomers" move here and then want Seattle to be "like New York" (it must have been my shoes), I vowed to keep a lid on my emotions, at least while standing in line waiting for a bagel.

I do this sometimes, let spill too soon a specific weakness that makes us human, makes us vulnerable, and, presto, when it is my new acquaintance's turn to reciprocate, she doesn't. Sometimes it's simply the price of opening up to someone.

Several tries-at-a-new-friend ago, while out with a woman I'd met at the gym, I brought up how PMS'y I was feeling that day and her reaction was, "I'm sorry, I don't go there in conversation." I'll never forget how uncomfortable her comeback made me, how incapable of understanding it I was. Wait, I wasn't talking about sex or anything. Women talk about this all the time, don't they? *Why did she invite me out then, to talk about the weather?* I could see nothing but the wall that went up between us. Who knows? Maybe she'd killed her lover and used the PMS defense. From the restroom, I called Larry on my cell, "It's just so boring. I swear I don't know what to say!"

What I meant was I didn't know, after her remark, how much to let out. It's such a fine balance, meeting someone new. I don't like total exposure, but holding back exhausts me.

"Make up some excuse and come home, then," my Larry said. And that's exactly what I did. The boat sank. I bailed.

If you don't think it took balls to walk away from that table, I beg to differ. It was one of those totally clear moments when you can be one or the other, a woman who wants to be liked ... or yourself. I knew exactly what to do: lie. "I'm sorry," I said. "I'm needed at home."

Then, of course, there is the flip side: leaving a potentially good friendship too early (she didn't email me back so the hell with her!).

The most important thing I try to practice these days is exactly the same thing I learned in my garden: I can't force something to take root; it has to adapt.

I also had to relearn a few truths about friendship that aren't likely to change along with my address: That break-ups happen between friends, they just do. Any other expectation of friendship is ... fiction.

In a dance class I used to teach, a woman I considered a friend was repeatedly late. But it wasn't her constant tardiness that upset me. It was that I kept expecting her to take the responsibility of her lateness in her own hands and say, "I'm really sorry I was late." She never did. And to me that crosses a friendship line. Even after I expressed not only my desire for timeliness, but my need for an apology, no easy thing to say to someone you really care about.

To this day, no single person has taught me more about the reality of passive-aggressive behavior than this woman. When we performed together, she'd pretend to cooperate then ignore what I, the artistic director, asked. When I began to see this pattern develop in other areas of our friendship, I walked away and never looked back. No part of me felt like I could count on her.

It was around that time, Jeane came into my life and I'd begun, sometimes unfairly, to compare a few of my other friendships to the ease I felt in her company, partly out of my friendship-research, partly out of gratefulness, and partly out of the relief of knowing what it felt like, finally, to be open.

Still, even when you find that special friend, the one you are open to, generous to — sometimes beyond your own expectations — no one is ever just who we need them to be all of the time, just as someone wise once said, most of all ourselves. And if you are anything like me, in the years it takes to integrate this truth into your life, you let yourself down from time to time.

Sometimes looking back at those times when I've let myself down hugely is so hard for me that I just can't bear it. And right now is one of those times. When I think about it, I've known I had to get to this next story eventually.

Years before I met Jeane or sat down to write this book, I experienced a parting that was, at the time — and likely will always be — my most confusing and painful friendship failure ever. It definitely made me the most afraid. Afraid the world was out to hurt my feelings. Afraid of trying to find a real friend again. More afraid I was unworthy of having one. But fear is how the world tries to crush you, right? It burrows into your psyche like a sliver.

"I hate this," I confessed to Larry.

"I know you do." Like most men, I suspect my husband doesn't entertain any too-deep thoughts about friendship do's and don'ts. He responds with a sheepish shrug, as if that is an adequate response. It isn't, of course. But it's the best my boy can do.

"How am I supposed to get over this without becoming a pessimist?"

"You will," he said adamantly. Now here is where I envy his certainty. My husband has always been a man clear about two things: that relationships ebb and flow. And being embedded in my love is enough. He's never been one of those men who are off to play sports or poker with his circle of pals. I'm his circle. But for me, and as much as I love him, he is not enough.

And I suppose he couldn't think of anything else to say because there was no right thing to say. I could pretend, but I knew there was no amount of his loyal comfort to change the fact that my friendship life felt downgraded again. It felt as if not only the physical energy was sucked out of me, but the spirit in me, too. I barely felt motivated enough to keep up with my work as a columnist let alone think about writing another book.

Slowly, painfully, I reach in. Here's my story:

Neither I nor my friend (I'll call R.) set out to hurt each other, but it's what we increasingly did over time. And I knew

I had to overcome the disappointment. Right from the first blow to my self-esteem, I knew. After we each changed direction and left us behind, neither of us bothering (or too afraid) to tell each other why, I knew. I also knew that if I could survive the pain of losing a friend I loved so much, I could do anything. "I thought she *got* me. Doesn't anyone *get* me?" I asked myself, woefully.

This again. At times these two words were hearable, at other times they shouted louder than my father used to when I refused to go to church. They reminded me how we have to learn the same things over and over sometimes, but brand-new each time.

"This feels awful," I confided in Jeane.

"Awful as in?"

"Awful as in awful."

She hesitated and then said, "Sometimes you have to get hurt really bad so you can start again. Feeling raw points you in the right direction because you don't plan, you just do." I knew she was referring to her first failed marriage, of a man who'd cheated on her repeatedly, but, as soon as she said those words, it felt as if my hurt opened huge before me like two arms I could walk into.

These words will hold me up I thought. And they did.

They still do.

Over time less and less confusion lay between how much I missed R. and myself.

Then my writer's mind said, "I'm going to write a book about all of this."

Uh oh, I thought. Because, until then, my friendship failures hadn't really registered on my list of favorite topics I wanted to write about.

But my mind likes getting her way.

Still, the idea felt wrong to me. Like cap sleeves on middle-aged women. But my writer's mind and I don't always share the same desires. "I'm going to choose to look the other way, then," I said.

R. and I met ten years ago, at a time when both of us were trying to fit in to the small town I made reference to earlier. She had recently moved to town. I'd been living there more than a decade, wondering whether I could stay.

It's easy to see why we became fast friends: We were both from the East Coast; both of us were married, both crazy about our husbands, and both wanting to escape living in a small town. That's what we called our desire to leave, *escape*, but, in our separate ways, we were both deeply entrenched in the community as well, our roots ran deep and we knew convincing our husbands, even ourselves, that the transition we craved — getting back to a city, she to New York and I to Seattle — was important for our personal development. So we embraced a friendship, sharing our likes and dislikes, our penchant for fashion, our appreciations, expectations, and mortifications. "Oh, my god!" R. blurted out one day, early in our relationship, "Don't you *dare* move away from here before I do!" We were, as the mother of all phrases goes, "two peas in a pod." City peas in a village pod.

But maybe — and I never gave this much thought until now — an integral part of our routine was competing for who would leave first. Not good.

Still, most women I know long for the kind of intimacy we shared. So why did this friendship end, and why was our parting so devastating to me? And why did it take so long for me to see my way through the shadowy hurt it cast over my days?

These questions are the culmination of everything I've written on the subject of friendship up to now. It's wonderful to realize a few answers. Or as close to answers as I ever get.

The one and only time R. and I sat down to try and confront what was up (or down) between us, why we were suddenly uncomfortable in each other's company rather than comforted, she said to me, "I don't want any of this to show up in your writing. Will you promise me that?"

At that meeting, in a restaurant overlooking the sea, I realized we were skilled at communicating when things were on a high note, but we had no clue how to find our way through how uncomfortable, now, we both found it to talk at all.

And I was surprised to find that I was not struck with sadness, at least not at first, but instead I felt defeated by the fact that neither of us was willing to do the hard work of saving what we'd built. How could such a mind-bending thing not wind its way into my writings? My work is the life inside me. Did she forget this along the way?

I think every writer has to face, sooner or later, the issue of privacy vs. a writer's right to write her life. Because nothing is more debilitating to a writer than feelings of loyalty, shameless as that sounds. The problem is that you want to be true to others and at the same time be true to your work. There is no way to marry these two opponents. If we try, our writing is boring and without risk. Who would want to read it? Nothing freezes a writer's mind more than promising someone this kind of allegiance. I knew the letdown of my friendship with R. was *the* friendship shake-up I'd have to overcome. And that doing so would show up in my writings somewhere. I just didn't know how or where yet. I was too busy thinking about everything to be the least bit reflective about it. But I knew it would pop up. Likely, in a big way. Oak trees rather than weeds.

The other thing I rediscovered in that restaurant? That hurt can drive me to do or say things very honestly and without regret.

I told her I could not promise where my writing would take me. It was meant to be a certainty, but it came out with the sniveling *un*certainly of a woman about to cry. I was groping. Which takes so much energy, feels irrepressibly inadequate, and always seems to miss the point. After I spoke, I felt a weird sensation. As if the plait between us tore free. Then it drifted away over our heads. How delicate our tie was, after all, I thought. I think back and wonder if it would have been possible to do more if I hadn't been so afraid.

Instead of being honest during the rest of the conversation, I withdrew. I sat there feeling sad about the prospect of losing my friend. I knew I'd be devastated tomorrow, probably as early as that night. Perhaps the saddest I've felt in a long, long while. I lost my friendship reference point. Everything felt haywire.

"The only way to the other side is through it," my friend Jackie said.

Which was exactly how it was.

But you know what? Before that, she was everything I was looking for in a friend. Our relationship was thrilling, the most intense friendship I've yet to experience. The irrepressible joy we felt in one another's company had a tranquilizing effect on me. I felt safe, understood, appreciated. There was much talk about how deeply we loved and needed each other.

But no one ever said that the most emotional friendships were the ones meant to last. I think we put too much yeast in the dough too quickly. Our friendship rose too fast and couldn't hold itself up. We fell flat.

But why, why, *why*?

For one thing, R.'s and my friendship was based on a similar want and a shared desire. Our grappling with a sense of place was nearly as huge as the bond other women experience when they share a pregnancy and motherhood. These friendships can sometimes be our most short-lived ties, even if, at first, they feel firm as the earth beneath us. What is that phrase my mom says all the time? *The harder they come, the quicker they fall.* Is that all it is? I don't know who came up with the catchall phase, or its match: *The larger the expectation, the bigger the disappointment.* But, in my own life, I finally understand how each applies, and why they live on.

Also, sustaining an intense-so-quickly friend can be a slippery slope if intensity is all you're after. As tricky as sustaining the same level of passion in a marriage.

Yet, in a marriage we are expected to work on it, expected to scream at each other recklessly from time to time. And carry on. But with friends we too often go silent when we're disappointed. I know I did.

Or worse, we gossip about our letdown to a third party. Again, guilty as charged. Even while I was blabbing, I knew this kind of gossip was a lazy means of not acting. But I was afraid to act. I was afraid R. would cut out on me. *Stop being afraid,* I told myself. But I wouldn't listen.

Meet the place of R. and me. Where I learned it's easy to love a friend. But hard to hold on to that love.

I remember how, aside from the excitement, there was this fearful awkwardness I could feel in her company due to the fact that I am nearly ten years older than she, which made it difficult to share parts of myself without sounding a tad condescending. Still, I liked that a younger friend found me so interesting.

Unfortunately, there was always this little voice in my head doubting she'd be in it for the long haul. Why this voice did not register a warning in some real way, I can't say. I suppose the mistake I can make, even now, is to think of those I admire as being better people than me.

Worse, sometimes, and this is not an easy thing to admit, I'd felt jealous of her younger-than-me-ness, a feeling that would creep up my spine against my will. The emotion that always feels small and inconsistent with whom I want to be, which also makes it all the more human. I thought about all of this a lot back then, and I began to wonder if anything short of having an affair could possibly be as neglectful to my marriage.

And here, nearly eight years after the fact, I can finally admit another fact of R. and me, something I struggled with and another reason why the friendship, to my mind, didn't make it: Just when I thought I'd finally found the friend I've been looking for all my life, that there was a whole new breed of friendship out there to tap into, a gold standard, it felt like R. replaced me.

One day it was us, the next, her life was aside-from-me. It happened quickly, way before I was able to make the shift, the first real sign that our age difference *did* matter. I could no longer shift my attachments, to people and places, so fast. Or wanted to. I was left asking myself, like her need to befriend me so intensely, did she need a new intensity, like a shopping fix, now that she and I were headed toward the second stage of friendship, commitment, flaws and all?

From what I could tell, R's new best friend found her fascinating, too. Yet, she was ten years younger than R., making her twenty years younger than me, a huge gap in our life-experience. "Too wide for me to cross," I told Larry, "there's no way I can re-enter my early thirties, no way I want to."

And, it seemed to me, a large part of their currency was gossip, the inside information of a small town. The kind of conversation that was not interesting to me. I'd outgrown it, felt uncomfortable around it. I became careful instead of open. I no longer confided in R. Instead I began feeding her little bits of my life. Just enough so I didn't have to go through the work of confronting her. Before I told her something private, a little voice in the back of my head asked me if I wanted her new friend to know this about me. And despite all that mental effort, when trust ends, there's really nowhere else to go.

My admiration for R. began to subside when I realized what I'd experienced was not intimacy, but her *talent* for intimacy, cultivated over many relationships and many years. And I began to question the level of sincerity in a talent like this, and whether closeness with whomever is next in line is the same as closeness with no one? After even more reflection, a huge part of me began to wonder if what happened between us had been a kind of preemptive strike on my part, to leave R. before she could leave me. It hadn't really felt like a strike, though. It felt like a miss.

I have no doubt I've omitted something. Something key. People are forever changing and I can never know all that R. was feeling. I'm not even fully aware of some of my own feelings. I do know that it's impossible to stick by someone who needs to move on. We stopped seeing each other in the spring of that year, but now I see how our friendship had stopped functioning way before that, and why I'd grown so anxious in the months leading up to that final meeting when everything changed; when I looked at our friendship from all sides and could see no side was the place for me.

Still, the transition from having R. in my life to not having her was not easy to make. It nearly crushed me. What a strange, unsocial year it was. I avoided anyone who knew her. To cope, I tried to play down my need for us, to suppress the hurt I'd feel every time her name was mentioned.

In the meantime, I *did* start to write about it, trying to squeeze my thoughts into these pages, finding the voice I needed but couldn't muster the day I met up with R. to talk about "us."

And after the critical first months of not seeing R., I realized I still had a lot of faith in friendship. Plus, I had other friends who would stay by my side even through the pitfalls. Ones maybe not so intense, but calmer. More reliable.

And, of course, I'd met Jeane. Even though I was hesitant, afraid of trying a new friendship again, another part of me was persistent. And Jeane is good at follow-through. And we became good together.

And I met Jackie. I re-connected with Libby and spent more time with Shanta and with other friends, too, because determination was, after all, something to do; it was its own kind of resolution.

Somewhere far from here, R. now lives in her cherished city of New York and I think a lot about how I'll always be grateful to her. Our friendship was a powerful teacher. It shed light on a part of myself I wanted to grow into, gave me permission to be more gregarious, freed up a huge part of me to be more open, showed me how wonderful it feels when someone acts so sincerely happy to see you.

Understanding what happened to us (from my viewpoint) didn't lessen the pain of its absence. Not right away. It took me a couple of years. Time is the healer, just as they say. And who knows, maybe one day I'll hear her name, feel nothing but a little wistfulness, and say, *R.? God, it was great to know her.*

Or, better still, maybe we'll come fully around again. Forgive. See ourselves through.

To this day, especially when I look at an old photograph of us, my impulse is to run back to her, to call or email her, even though I'm pretty sure of what this says about my stubborn inability to learn from the past.

Pretty sure, but not completely.

FORGIVING — *for R.*

Every so often you rush back
into memory. Who knows why?

A particular curve to a cheekbone,
a stranger's mouth fans into a smile
too full of joy to ignore
and your face floods in.

I can manage, though,
keep you from splashing the rest of my life
the way you used to. You could say I lived my life
back then soaking wet.

Now, I'm able to balance the remembering
with no hands while riding a bicycle
without spilling a drop.

I can do this, quiet myself
through a string of winters
till cold backs off, the air appeased
with warmth, forgiveness
no longer a deep, sharp stab so huge
it pins me to the floor.

Instead, something softer.
Twilight, perhaps. Or a rosebush
thriving under a cedar.

Even with their own set of impossibilities:
the insistence of darkness,
or leaves black-spotted.

Still, sunlight always returns, no?

And the rosebush, even after winter's freeze,
is heavy with buds again.

So you see. As things turned out,
I needn't have worried so much.

SEVEN

Closing Thoughts

"Oh, the comfort, the inexpressible comfort of feeling safe with a person; having neither to weigh thoughts nor to measure words but to pour them all out, just as it is, chaff and grain together, knowing that a faithful hand will take and sift them, keeping what is worth keeping, and then, with the breath of kindness, blow the rest away."

— ANN CURRY

It's a summer day. In our small, one-storied cottage in Port Townsend, all the windows and doors are open. Walking past, there's a man wearing a fedora whose name I don't know but who has walked by here for years. Next door a construction worker takes a lunch break. He's reading the newspaper, probably the sports section. The faint acrid smell of the lumber mill in the distance mixes with the sweet-sour tang of the sea. And there's the scent of the rosemary I planted when we first moved here two decades ago. A sprig of it graces my sill.

I walk into my tiny office. This is a familiar yet altogether new room for me. The chair I painted white and the built-in desk I wrote my first books on are fixtures in my memory, true, but I come to them anew now — a thought that feels me with awe. Reverence comes easily to me lately. A gust of warm air moves through my writing nook. When I think about it, a lot of things moved through me here.

How excited I was about living here then! It was our first home, our first community as a couple. After moving in, I got started: shrubs I planted grew into trees, acquaintances grew into long-standing friendships, my love of dance grew into directing a dance company, my passion for writing grew into seven collections of poetry, and a newer desire, writing essays, grew into regular columns for newspapers, magazines, and radio.

Initially the essays were a way of my waking up to everything following September 11th when the world's tensions reverberated so deep I couldn't seem to find, writing poetry, the mood I needed to transcend my fear. I needed to expand beyond the conciseness poetry demands and more permission to laugh and poke a little fun. This isn't going to win me any poetic friends, but most of the poets I know are ... sort of dour. A few of them scare me.

I was tired, too, of being a writer at the periphery, which is where poetry, unfortunately, exists in our society. I wanted more people to read my work.

And this feeling, one of being in the outfield, began to chip away at how I felt about living in a small town — Port Townsend lies at the end of a peninsula at the end of an even larger peninsula — and the isolation I once craved, which is also the town's greatest charm, began to weigh on my peace of mind. And it's why I needed to leave.

So off I went.

Looking back, I now see how much I didn't know about myself in those early days in Port Townsend, and yet, by re-reading the paragraphs above, it's clear how much I was certain of, too. And this certainty is what drove my work and my desires, along with the pressures of each. It still does.

I've always defined a huge part of my life by setting goals, which is easy, and then attaining them, which is the hard part. "You came out of the womb disciplined," my mom says. She says this because she doesn't want to attribute too much of me to my father, her ex, an immigrant from Italy, who showed me daily how a rigorous work ethic, a firm belief in physical action, and the need to rise after the knock-downs, eventually gets you to where you want to be.

That's life, that's life. That's what all the people say. I'm riding high in April, shot down in May. Those are the lyrics that rang out of my father's bathroom when he was showering or shaving, his favorite Sinatra song. This tipped me off that there would be some blows.

And there have been.

As much as I like to think I've intentionally shaped my life — my long-standing marriage, a career that sustains me, and friendships I delight in — I believe much of it was formed by my background. I could see in my father's eyes all he wanted to accomplish. For him, all that lay ahead of him in America was digging in and working hard. And, like most immigrants, he was happy to have the work.

I learned a great deal from his straightforward approach to life. And it seems important to say just what those lessons were in this closing chapter.

Everyone I know wants to visit Italy and be charmed by the past. And yet Europeans are far less enamored by the past then we Americans think. For one thing, they seldom romanticize it the way we do. Since World War II, they've worked hard to live in the present. How else could they move forward and dig themselves out of such a war-torn past? The present is all my family wants to think or talk about. Most Americans don't seem to understand that this is why Europeans linger over those five-course meals, savoring the ease, holding on to the present as if to a mane. Not wanting to fall off the crest they've worked so hard to achieve, knowing first-hand how far civilization can sink once a descent begins.

I have only to close my eyes to see how this live-in-the-present way of life became my own. Every time I experience a loss or need to move ahead, when the past feels like a tide moving against me, I remember my father's discipline, and I shift my focus to the present until I can see nothing ahead but the future. It's invigorating. The past is an anchor, certainly. And, like an anchor, it can hold you back.

Now, for the downside of being a daughter of a man from a machismo culture (and the world is full of them): I was expected to obey him no matter what. I suppose rebelling against this expectation from an early age helped me, more than anything else, tap into my strengths. First I had to rebel against my father's authority, then my (mostly male) teachers' expectations for girls, later as a woman, a wife, and certainly as a poet and writer.

And though I wasn't fully aware of this from the beginning, I see how my past turned out to be helpful in writing this book. I spent some time researching the European sense of commitment to others — Europe is not a culture addicted to the next new thing as much as America is; most have far less disposable income, and live their entire lives in close proximity to family and age-old friends — in order to understand how another trait helped form who I am today, and why perhaps my own friendship disappointments can fester under my skin for so long. That trait: loyalty.

I am loyal. In the Old World sense. I've remained loyal to my marriage for thirty years, to friends willing to weather the storms together, to my writing always, even when words seem too empty for the work at hand.

When I hear people criticize their spouses or their so-called friends behind their backs, or attempt a goal once or twice before giving up and moving on, I want to ask, *what is it you are after here*? Where is your commitment, your dedication, your loyalty to yourself, your work, and others?

My only wish is that while my family was setting an admirable, loyal, responsible example, they could have enjoyed life more. But maybe one can never achieve ease once war has penetrated your life and stripped you of your faith in peace. But that's another subject.

Or is it?

I think this is why — it *is* why — I moved as far west as possible, married a man whose family goes back three generations in "laid-back" California, and why my West Coast friends have had such an influence on me: because I prefer looking at life through the eyes of those who aren't running from something, and to be moored to those with something other than getting ahead in mind.

But this doesn't lessen the effect of what was passed down to me by my family.

Nevertheless, loyalty is not an easy topic to tackle. Especially when the next new thing seems like our culture in a nutshell. This is terrifically liberating in many instances, and why I left the fold of my family to move to the opposite coast in the first place: to experience the freedom of a new city like Seattle. But when it comes to friendships, it also makes me wonder, all over again, if we know what it's like to be loyal to anything ... other than desire.

It seems I'm always of two minds, straddling two worlds: old world loyalty vs. new world freedom from loyalty's constraints. And this dichotomy makes me feel rootless in so many ways.

When I look up from my keyboard to consider what I just wrote, here's what I think: Writing is where I find myself, where I'm most at home. On days when I don't know what I'm doing or where I'm supposed to head, writing talks me through. Or sometimes it's simply the sound of my fingers clicking away at the keys that brings me back until I can hear the woman inside me say *there you are*! In the same breath, she also says *this is as much a home as anywhere. And it is a solid place.*

This makes me think, in relation to my friendships, I probably would have ended up just about where I am today no matter what. Because trusting this voice, this home *within* took me a lot of time. My lifetime so far. In the mean time, I've had to wade through all the pitfalls and insecurities of my relationships year by year.

And as the pages of this particular book came together, I thought so much more about how it has always felt like my fate to be a writer, to use my personal life as my work, without knowing, when I was a young writer, that there was a whole school of thought to my way of working. What I believe, in the way others trust religion, is what Carl Jung and many other writers have advocated all along: that what's most profoundly personal is also most universal.

It was a comfort to learn there are entire schools of thought that match my way of thinking: Connecting with the small daily-ness of self is the biggest thing there is. Especially when so many of my newspaper and magazine editors have tried (without success) to sway me toward the journalistic (leave yourself out of the story) approach to writing rather then the intimacy I like to slide into my work. As I wrote before, but it bears repeating: *Nothing is more satisfying than connecting to what matters in the mind of another. I write to connect: others to others, others to me, me to me. These are good fits.*

Back to my cottage by the sea:

In the first months after moving to the city, I couldn't visit this cottage, or the younger woman I was, without waves of confusion flooding my insides. My past would crash into my future; my present would get crushed to bits in between. I knew I had to get through it, that there was no shortcut to feeling solid on my feet again. That I couldn't cheat.

Yet these days, two years since I left living in this small town full-time, I like returning. In the city, each day is full of work, friends, responsibilities. To counter that fullness, I enjoy pulling up the weeds growing around this cottage as if tending to my history. I find the cottage gives me just enough of the kind of refuge and anchor I need. It keeps me in touch with living on the ground where everything in nature is shifting, quite visibly, all the time. One bush will thrive while another turns three shades of brown. The lavender re-seeds itself without my slightest effort, but the roses are dying, I can't keep up with the aphids and black spots no matter what.

All of this is entirely different from the acceleration I see each day in the city: man's need to build higher and grander. Yet, both worlds remind me, in much the same way, how there is no stillness. I once believed, with the enthusiasm of an evangelist, that living in this small town would sustain me forever, that the friends I made in my late twenties would be my confidantes for life, that I'd write poetry forever, and never venture into other genres. How fluid life really is. How ever-changing. For who, given half a chance, would choose to drag along the weight of their former selves, unchallenged, for the rest of their lives?

Coming here now, I feel how hungry I was as a younger woman. And how I learned to feed myself.

Coming here, too, reminds me of the somewhere in between I struggled in for so long: wanting the change I needed, which was necessary, and making the change, which can take so much longer. There was a lot of work that needed doing first.

Now I can see all the connections between the woman I was here, and my current strengths in my life, work, and relationships.

And I can feel inside the younger woman I was when I began this book, when I thought losing my best friend would undo me.

Here, in this yard by the sea, I live a triumph.

A week later, I wrote this: Changing my home, my career, my relationships required so much work and risk and double-daring myself. Only now, years later, do my choices make any sense. They are belated aware-nesses.

In Anne Morrow Lindbergh's *A Gift from the Sea,* she addresses these "aware-nesses" so well that I feel humbled even bringing them up again.

There is one chapter in which I highlighted nearly every sentence when I was only a few friendship-heartaches past the age of twenty. Looking at those pages now, I remember how I drank them in, thirsty for Lindbergh's explanations as if my life depended on it. I wanted to *know*. Everything. And I wanted to be reassured by an older woman who was a writer that my friendship goofs and hurts weren't unusual but part of the ordinary.

Here is the passage I underlined in blue ink, and then, as if wanting it to glow even brighter, again in orange highlighter. It just fills me with wonder how, reading these time-worn pages of a book published in 1955, it still reads as if it were released today. She stresses that becoming the women we want to be demands we continue to dare, to hone in, to simplify:

It is true, of course, the original relationship is very beautiful. Its self-enclosed perfection wears the freshness of a spring morning. Forgetting about the summer to come, one often feels one would like to prolong the spring of early love, when two people stand as individuals, without past or future, facing each other. One resents any change, even though one knows that transformation is natural and part of the process of life and its evolution. The early ecstatic stage of relationship cannot continue always at the same pitch. It either moves to another phase of growth which one should not dread, but welcome as one welcomes summer after spring. Both will feel the change in the early relationship and hunger nostalgically for its original pattern as life goes on and becomes more complicated. Obviously some relationships can never make the transition or be recovered. It is not just a question of different needs to be understood and filled. In their changing roles the two may have grown in different directions or at different rates of speed. Some relationships are an end in themselves. A brief episode may have been all they could achieve.

It's Friday, the 13th of June, 2008.

"How can it be that I finish my book on Friday the 13th?" I ask Larry, slightly panicked.

"Maybe that's a good thing," he says and just sort of nods his head.

Yes. It feels like it is, somehow. This supposedly bad luck day is the perfect metaphor for all the ungrounded fears that put this book into motion.

I like how it feels to sit here having a timeout with what it feels like to have rolled up my sleeves and ploughed through to the end of a book after years of talking about it, putting it off, brainstorms, and exhausting work.

And yet, far from feeling elated, I feel overcome. And a little sad. Much like it feels, I'm reminded befittingly, to have a cherished friendship end: part relief, part regret. Especially about what I wasn't capable of doing or saying.

I wonder if other writers, during the last weeks of finishing a book, hear a voice. A testy, mean voice. Right now mine keeps belittling my writing a book about friendship, while more worldly heartbreaks are everywhere: War, famine, illness, poverty ... the list is endless.

I don't know what to make of this voice that finds an easy way into my vulnerabilities because, knowing the end of my book is near, I start to dread the empty-nesty feeling. Larry, who has seen me through this many times, says it's my "in-between." For the next few weeks, I'll not only be in between writing projects, I'll be in between selves. Half of me will feel like I still need the discipline, the focus, those aggravating sentences that won't say what I need them to. The other half will be glad to be rid of the whole damn friendship topic because I'm beginning to fear that the only place in the world I know myself well is right here, cloistered in my office.

This must be what it felt like for my friend Max to leave her youngest son, Ben, at the bus stop for the first time. And what she'll probably feel when she leaves him off at college for the last. Anyway you slice it, it's an empty nest.

So I'm going to pop some corn, settle down in front of the TV, and watch three movies in a row.

"Tomorrow I'll think of a way to finish," I say aloud to myself.

"Let's *hope* so," she says back. "Because I'm done here."

I am not the woman now that I was when I lived in a sea-side village, or when I moved to Seattle new to its fibers. Neither am I the woman I was when I started this book, the woman who wanted to write about friendship. I can't possibly ingest one more kernel of friendship-info. My motivations have changed.

Still, I'm grateful. Because slowly, but not reluctantly, I can clearly see my part in my friendship births as well as their demises. This book took its sweet time to help me make sense of these changes. And it may seem otherwise, but it's not been easy work to reveal myself on these pages. There were days I felt like my head was going to bust open from all the hurt feelings and because I couldn't seem to resolve one thing.

But it's been necessary.

And, finally, settling.

About the Author

Mary Lou Sanelli is the author of eight other books including *Falling Awake*. She works as a writer/speaker/performer. For information regarding her various titles, readings and talks, please visit www.marylousanelli.com.

Aequitas Books is an imprint of *Pleasure Boat Studio: A Literary Press* which focuses on nonfiction books with philosophical or sociological themes.

To see backlist contact our website
www.pleasureboatstudio.com